Overcoming Common Problems

Coping with SAD

Fiona Marshall
and
Peter Cheevers

sheldon**PRESS**

Published in Great Britain in 2002 by
Sheldon Press
1 Marylebone Road
London NW1 4DU

British Library Cataloguing-in-Publication Data

A catalogue record for this book is available from the British Library

ISBN 0–85969–873–4

Typeset by Deltatype Limited, Birkenhead, Merseyside
Printed in Great Britain by Biddles Ltd
www.biddles.co.uk

Contents

For all who would like more light in their lives.

Acknowledgements

We are indebted to all the pioneers of light therapy and research into SAD: Dr John Ott, Norman Rosenthal and Jacob Liberman; to all the research done at the National Institute for Mental Health, Washington, USA; to research done at the University of Basel, Switzerland; at University of British Columbia Faculty of Medicine, Vancouver; as well as to work by Professor Chris Thompson and Dr Ian Rodin at the Royal South Hants Hospital, Southampton. We are also indebted to the inspirational work of Primrose Cooper on light and Kathleen DesMaisons on nutrition.

Thanks also to all who shared their experiences with us, including Ben Mankowich.

Introduction

'For the rest of my life I will reflect on what light is', wrote Albert Einstein in 1917. Light, the source of life, is at the core of our culture. From romantic candles to the full intensity of holiday sunshine, the power of light to affect our mood and wellbeing is tacitly accepted by society.

It can be no coincidence that light features in so many of our religious festivals, from Diwali to Ramnavmi, the Hindu festivals of light, and gives such inspiration to the millions of children around the world celebrating Christmas, which despite its Christian nature, is based on ancient pagan celebrations of the return of sunlight after the winter solstice.

Yet many doctors now agree that the last two or three generations of people are the first to be spending at least three quarters of daily life under artificial light. In times gone by, survival dictated that many work outside or near to windows during daylight. Over the past few decades, however, those of us in the West have been spending more and more of our time indoors.

In most cases, we wake indoors, breakfast under artificial light, get into our interior-lit car or train, arrive at our fluorescently lit office, eat in the subdued light of the canteen or restaurant and, even if we manage a lunchtime walk, in many of our major cities, tall buildings shade out the light. So, for modern-day city dwellers, especially those living in northern latitudes, the sun is not seen very much for large chunks of the year – the exception being the overkill doses on the annual two-week holiday.

The result of all this – our changed level of exposure to light – is the extraordinary increase in the documentation of SAD, which stands for seasonal affective disorder. An estimated 1 in 20 people suffer from SAD, though it must be remembered that many will not bother to record what they regard as a normal condition of life – feeling low in the winter. Indeed, changes in energy, appetite, mood and sleep may be seen in most people in winter to some extent. But for those with SAD they are severe enough to interfere significantly with normal living.

In the US, an estimated 10 per cent of the population suffer from SAD, and this may be a contributing factor in the startlingly high figure of one in three cases of depression recorded on the North American continent.

However, there is hope. With the acceptance of SAD as a treatable disorder, people, encouraged by the availability of knowledge in our information age, are beginning to ask questions about light and health. Not just how lack of light affects our psychological wellbeing, but more fundamental, even revolutionary, questions. Could there be links between our modern screening out of light and the increase in many diseases? Why are so many degenerative diseases more common in Western societies? Diseases such as hardening of the arteries, senile dementia, multiple sclerosis and high blood pressure are very common, but is it just diet and lack of exercise that are to blame? Could there be a link between lack of light and these conditions? Could light therapy improve such things as hyperactivity, infertility and respiratory infection?

These ideas go well beyond the scope of this book, but the fact that such questions are being looked into suggests that SAD may only be the tip of the iceberg as far as health is concerned. The effects of sunlight on mood and health – the subject of much research earlier in the last century – had remained of marginal medical interest until relatively recently, from the 1980s onwards. Since then, serious research work has been done into SAD (and other conditions – studies suggest that therapeutic use of light is of benefit in a wide range of situations, including schools and zoos!).

So, is the only hope to emigrate to a sunnier climate? While a winter holiday may be a great help, light therapy is a highly effective treatment and much more easily available than it used to be. In addition, there is a wealth of ways in which you can help yourself, including diet and exercise, which this book will also explore.

The latest research into the condition suggests that it is the result of an abnormality in the function of serotonin, the hormone which wakes us up and lifts our mood. Serotonin levels are known to fluctuate and be at their lowest in the winter. Serotonin also influences melatonin – the hormone responsible for making us fall asleep – and these links will also be explored further in this book, along with ways to boost serotonin levels.

People have somehow managed to endure SAD for millennia

without treatment. However, as you will find, there are many options available for the sufferer of SAD. Seasonal affective disorder can be treated. It is hoped that this book will help sufferers of SAD, carers and families and be a source of support and reference.

1
What is SAD?

'Winter is a disease', wrote the nineteenth-century French poet Alfred de Musset, and many people with SAD would wholeheartedly agree with him. Those lowering grey skies seem to invade every corner of your being, flattening all hopes and aspirations and mocking all those old summer dreams of happiness. However, this winter disorder can be treated. You can start today, now, and – unless you are very depressed – you may be able to do much of it yourself. While your doctor may have a part to play in treating SAD, another condition or your general health, there is a great deal that you can do for yourself to shift SAD, without a huge amount of effort. It can be something as simple as putting down this book, walking over to the window and taking a long look at the sky. Even on dark days, there will be around ten times more light in the sky than in your room, and absorbing it via your eyes can start to lift your mood (this will be explained in more detail later in this book).

Winter depression – also known as 'light hunger', 'grey sky syndrome' and 'cabin fever' – is not a figment of the imagination, nor is it a new fad. Psychiatrists have known for a long time that mood and emotional disorders can be seasonal. In 1845 there are records of patients with symptoms that we now know to be SAD, with accompanying doctors' recommendations that the patients winter in sunny Italy instead of Belgium. Later, in the nineteenth century, a ship's doctor observed that his crew was becoming increasingly lethargic during the dark days of an Arctic winter and he recommended that their languor be treated with light.

Awareness of seasonal rhythms goes back well before this. Hippocrates, in the fifth century BC, felt that prospective doctors should first get a thorough understanding of seasonal changes and corresponding changes in people and animals. 'Some natures are well or ill-adapted for summer, and some for winter. Such diseases as increase in the winter ought to cease in the summer', he wrote. 'The doctor too must treat disease with the conviction that each of them is powerful in the body according to the season which is most conformable to it.'

Winter is well known for its effects on health. Death from all causes peaks in January. Hospitalization for depression increases dramatically in the winter months. Family doctors expect to be busier in winter, with an increase in general referrals. This increase is not just due to viral infections, but also to complaints whose causes are sometimes less easy to diagnose – fatigue, sleep problems and odd aches and pains that may not have a physiological basis. Symptoms like these often indicate SAD.

Despite its long history, the term SAD has only been with us for the last few decades, making it a comparatively recent addition to the list of conditions that can be clinically diagnosed and one that is not fully known or understood. SAD often meets with scepticism, from lay people and the medical profession alike. 'Who really likes winter?', as one doctor said. However, for those going through the misery of SAD, the condition is very real. Many people with the condition know they will feel better when the weather changes and just hang on until spring. They often do not seek treatment and therefore are not registered as sufferers. They may find the depression debilitating – and many do – but they manage. Some, however, do not. For people with full-blown SAD – about 2 to 3 per cent of the population – the disorder can be life-shattering. The serious depression experienced causes them to withdraw from social activities and lose interest in their usual lifestyle. As symptoms worsen with the deepening winter, they may lose their job or an important relationship or drop out of school or college because they can't function. It is vital to take SAD seriously, and, if you do think you are suffering from any kind of depression, consult your doctor as soon as possible. Depression is treatable. It is worth consulting your doctor anyway if you have any worrying symptoms before you assume it is SAD as you may be suffering from some other condition, such as chronic fatigue or a viral infection, which can also be treated.

What is SAD?

I don't mind winter so long as the days are bright – it's those dull cloudy days that get me down.
I always tend to eat more when it's cold.
I can't wait for the spring.

I'm a summer person, definitely.

Seasonal affective disorder (SAD) – defined as depression caused by lack of natural light – is now recognized as a condition by the World Health Organization (WHO). What, though, makes it different from the feelings expressed above, feelings that most people share to some extent?

Many of us undergo seasonal variations in mood, energy, appetite and sleep in winter and summer. It is not surprising to prefer salads in summer and warming hearty dishes in winter. It is common to be more energetic and active in spring than in the depths of winter – indeed, society has organized (in the UK at least) what amounts to a two-week shutdown in the form of Christmas and the New Year in the darkest part of winter. Many people tend to feel a bit down as the dull winter days wear on and on into January and February, and the first days of real spring sunshine usually bring a general lightening of mood.

The difference with SAD, however, is that what is experienced is an exaggerated version of these mild seasonal blues and, in particular, that, while most people cope with these feelings, those with SAD find their ability to cope is seriously affected – sometimes disabled – by the condition. Here is what Alison, a 32-year-old teacher, says about SAD.

> Disabling is the word. You are literally less able to carry out normal life – working, driving, seeing friends. Your body goes out of your control because of the bingeing on food that is such a feature of SAD. It's not really about snuggling up early with a hot water bottle and enjoying it. You feel you're only living half a life because you end up sleeping so much while other people are out there getting on with it. SAD is such an unproductive use of a life – you really feel life is slipping past you while you struggle on, waiting for spring.
> *Alison*

This book deals with the best-known form of SAD – a type of winter depression that tends to begin as the days shorten between September or October and lasts until March or April. In keeping with the shortening days, it is often worst between December to February.

SAD has been divided into two levels of intensity.

- **Sub-SAD** or **sub-syndromal SAD** This affects an estimated 30 per cent of people and is when 'normal' winter feelings become more noticeable and begin to affect everyday life. This may overlap with the condition known as 'winter vegetative pattern', where people's energy levels are lowered but their mood is not affected.
- **Full-blown SAD** This is when the depression becomes more disabling, affecting life to the extent that the person finds it difficult to carry out normal activities, such as going out.

There are different kinds of SAD, too, each with these levels of intensity.

Summer SAD

No cure for the summertime blues, it is said. Seasonal variations don't just apply to winter. An estimated 10 per cent of seasonal depression takes place in the summer. This may be triggered or intensified by excessive heat and humidity.

Little is known about summer SAD. One possibility is that some people actually receive less light in hot weather because they spend more time indoors sheltering from the sun and/or wear sunglasses when they go out, thus effectively blocking the light from their eyes.

The holiday blues

SAD is sometimes confused with Christmas depression, when, instead of roasting chestnuts by the fire and exchanging gifts in an atmosphere of cosiness and warmth, you may be alone and lonely or at bitter loggerheads with the people whom fate has picked out as your family.

There are many causes for holiday blues – sadness that the present can never match up to childhood memories of the event, feelings of being trapped in childhood patterns with parents you have long outgrown, feeling isolated from your usual activities and friends, just feeling isolated, disgust at the commercialism of Christmas and so on. Such feelings may exist with or without SAD.

Of course if you do have winter depression, you may not find Christmas a cheerful big day and will continue to be depressed well after the event. If you do not have SAD, but do suffer from the holiday blues, you probably find you feel better once the last bits of tinsel have been taken down and you are safely back at work or any other usual routine.

What causes SAD?

Causes are looked at in more detail in Chapter 4, but, briefly, as well as lack of light, SAD is thought to be caused by a biochemical imbalance in the brain, featuring a lack of the brain chemical serotonin. In winter, some northern locations only have around 8 hours of daylight – as opposed to 16 hours at the peak of summer – and some people with certain brain chemistries seem to be particularly sensitive to this reduction.

What happens is that light, as well as allowing us to see, is used by the body for a variety of metabolic purposes, just as food and water are. Entering the body via the eyes, light stimulates the pineal gland to secrete substances that regulate the human biological clock. This in turn influences sleeping, eating, activity levels and moods – all of which are affected by SAD. In some people, the pineal gland seems to need more outside help in terms of light stimulus in order to function effectively.

Many SAD sufferers come from a family where a parent or close relative suffers from SAD and some research suggests that there may be a hereditary factor in at least 30 per cent of cases of SAD.

Emotional stress may trigger the depression, but there may be no obvious trigger. Everything can be going well in someone's life, but when winter comes, their mood plummets.

SAD symptoms are sometimes explained away by memories of trauma in autumn, especially starting or returning to school. However, the SAD symptoms typically last five or six months – much longer than the initial start of a new school year. Also, perhaps more importantly, depression from trauma does not usually respond to light treatment, as does SAD.

How do I know if it's SAD?

The basic hallmark of SAD is a feeling of overwhelming depression recurring every year during the winter and occasionally during the summer. Symptoms (discussed more fully in Chapter 3) may include extreme tiredness and cravings for carbohydrates, as well as sadness, anxiety, irritability, headaches, weight gain, joint stiffness, lack of interest in sex and lack of concentration and motivation. Those affected may have difficulty thinking and making decisions or carrying out work and social activities (all symptoms of major depression).

In milder cases, some people may just feel that their energy has dropped, but experience relatively little depression. People usually feel much better in spring and summer when their mood will typically lift, with around 30 per cent of people experiencing a definite 'high' or feeling of elation in spring that, for some, can spill over into mania.

According to the criteria laid down by the WHO, the main point to check for is that the depression is seasonal – that is, it starts and ends at particular times of year (usually autumn and spring).

Medical authorities seem to agree that, for a diagnosis of SAD to be made, the following symptoms will be experienced:

- the depression lasts for a period of at least 60 days between October/November and March/May;
- there must be three episodes, two of which are consecutive;
- seasonal depression must outnumber other depressions by three to one;
- there should be no environmental factors or stresses, such as being unemployed or isolated from friends in winter.

SAD can be just as severe and serious as other kinds of depression and, like them, if left untreated can wreck the person's quality of life even, in extreme cases, posing a risk of suicide. On the positive side, it is important to remember that depression does pass and seasonal depression, by its very nature, is likely to lift with the end of winter. Meanwhile, there is a lot that can be done to alleviate the suffering, which this book will explore in later chapters.

How common is SAD?

- SAD may affect anyone and begin at any age, but is believed to start mainly between the ages of 20 and 40, with the main sufferers being women in their 20s and 30s.

6

- More women are affected than men – in some areas the proportions are as high as three to one.
- It has also been documented in children and in the elderly.
- SAD has been linked with other conditions, such as PMS (premenstrual syndrome.)
- Doctors in the UK estimate that 1 in 20 people have been diagnosed as having SAD. This figure doesn't take into account those sufferers who have not been diagnosed, of course, so it is possible that this figure is the tip of a vast iceberg. According to reports for the NIMH in Bethseda, America, approximately 10 million Americans have SAD and, if you include sub-SAD, it is estimated that more than 30 million North Americans suffer to some degree from winter depression.

While SAD has been documented throughout the northern and southern hemispheres, it is extremely rare in those living within 30 degrees of the equator, where daylight hours are long, constant and extremely bright. It is more common in northern latitudes, with people in Scandinavia, Alaska and Iceland being most at risk. The northern parts of the United States and Europe typically have higher rates of alcoholism, depression, family violence and suicide than places further south that get more light. In the northernmost parts of the United States, SAD strikes nearly 10 per cent of people, as opposed to 1.4 per cent in the southernmost states. Equally, in Canada, around 600,000 people are known to suffer from SAD, according to a survey in Toronto published in the *Canadian Journal of Psychiatry*. It was found that about 3 per cent of the population have seasonal depression – a higher percentage than other well-researched diseases, such as schizophrenia and obsessive compulsive disorder.

Alison's story

Alison, 32, is a teacher from London who eventually decided to move to Brazil. Here is how she describes her experience of SAD.

I first experienced what I now know to be SAD in the autumn in my early 20s. It was my first job, I was miles from home and had just ended a relationship, so I had reasons for feeling down and blamed my depression on life events. But, the next autumn, my life situation was much better, and I was surprised when my mood started to plummet again as winter approached with the low grey skies and the endless rain. I kept thinking I should be able to pull myself together and snap out of it, but I couldn't.

That winter, I put on a stone and a half and I knew I wasn't eating to keep the cold out! I was so tired and demotivated I could barely get out of bed. I was frightened of life and of going out and just wanted to put my head under the covers and hide and cry. I didn't realize it at the time, but my thinking was very depressed and morbid – endless thoughts of dying, of time passing. I kept thinking that I was going to die anyway one day, so what was the point of living? It was quite terrifying. I was also very picky with the kids at school and every little thing seemed to get on top of me.

This went on for a couple more years. When spring came, I'd be fine – my energy would return, the weight would drop off and I would be happy and active again. Then, in late autumn, it would all begin again, and I began to blame myself. I felt I was lazy or not organized enough. I was acutely anxious in that I felt life was sliding past me and I was on the outside, missing out. I didn't have the perspective on my situation to see how my depression was cyclical and varied with the seasons . . . until I took a winter holiday in the sun.

The difference in how I felt was so striking – and happened so quickly, within a day or two of arriving – that I finally made the connection. Once I had that handle on it, things fell into place quite quickly. My own doctor had never heard of SAD, but I researched it myself on the Internet and invested in a lightbox. Most of my friends thought I was mad, but when they saw the difference in my moods, they became grudgingly convinced.

Whereas previously I had found it difficult to live a normal life in the winter due to severe depression, suddenly I was able to go out with my colleagues in the evening for a meal or a concert again; I ran a lunchtime and after-school club, and I no longer fell asleep at 8 p.m.!

The lightbox provided me with just enough light to get me going again. I would still feel a bit down, but it was nowhere near as bad. I made friends with a Brazilian girl, Marta, who also

suffered from SAD, visited Brazil with her and decided to live there for a while and teach English. I know not everyone is in a position to do this, but I think it will be worth it.
Alison

Not everyone is so affected by SAD that it makes sense to move countries. However, Alison's story shows what an impact SAD can have on people's lives and – equally important – that SAD can be tackled and the experience may even push you into new ways of living and being that are far more enriching than you might have imagined.

2

Sunlight starvation

'There is no area of our mental and bodily functioning that the sun does not influence. We were not designed to hide from it in houses, offices, factories and schools', says SAD expert Dr Damien Downing – and he might have added cars.

Sunlight and good-quality indoor lighting are often overlooked components of health. Yet, light is literally life-giving and nothing would exist without it. Light helps the body to produce vitamin D, absorb calcium and manufacture certain hormones and neurotransmitters key to mood and energy level, such as norepinephrine and serotonin. Sunlight is known to trigger a number of biological processes, just like food and water. Lack of light is the key factor in SAD.

For centuries our work had been governed by the amount of daylight available. Although this is still true for farmers and rural communities, in Western industrialized societies, we live indoors, are educated indoors and work indoors, spending more and more time away from the sun. Sunlight is still sunlight even on the cloudiest day.

At the beginning of the twentieth century, more than 70 per cent of Americans worked outside. Today, an estimated 38 million North Americans suffer the effects of malillumination, causing poor work conditions, which can result in less energy and productiveness. The amount of outside light we receive is less than has been the case for any other previous generation.

In the UK, the growth of rickets was directly linked to lack of daylight due to crowded buildings and smog in cities, even though the value of sunlight and fresh air in preventing rickets had been noted in 1822. Recently, there has been growing scientific interest in the therapeutic powers of sunlight and of artificial light for a wide range of ills, from obesity to cancer. Claims made for the healing power of sunlight, in some cases, go back as far as the ancient Greeks, though more research is certainly needed before your GP will prescribe you a holiday in the sun!

How much light do we need? Health experts have suggested that we may have a 'minimum daily requirement' of full-spectrum light from half an hour to two hours a day. This seems minimal indeed if you consider that we evolved outside. The brightness of light is measured in lux:

- 1 lux is around a single candle's light;
- around 200 to 700 lux, is normal room light indoors;
- about 100,000 lux is a sunny sky at midday – a cloudy day is around a third of that;
- around 0.00001 lux – the faintest light – is starlight without the moon shining

Light treatment for SAD (discussed more fully in Chapter 7) starts at 2,500 lux. This seems to be the minimum amount of light that is required to have a positive effect. New devices for light therapy tend to be more powerful than this. All the same, if you compare lux values indoors with those outdoors, it is easy to see how light starvation happens. Even a cloudy, grey winter's day gives ten times more light than the best-lit office.

Healing sunlight

Over the past four million years, modern man is believed to have evolved from the Olduvai Gorge in East Africa, close to the equator. We evolved outdoors, in sunlight. Anthropologists believe that the human race has spread out from this one source to cover the Earth and have adapted accordingly – or not. Could SAD be related to the fact that, as a global race, we were designed to live in a sunny climate?

There is a growing body of scientific opinion that supports the idea that our modern lack of not just sunlight, but also daylight is damaging our psychological wellbeing and our general health. Is SAD just the tip of the iceberg?

Because exposure to full-spectrum light has an important influence on the system, it is speculated that it can reduce the risks of many diseases, including cancer. There is no conclusive scientific evidence for the benefits of 'solar therapy', but research certainly suggests that we should all get more daylight and more sunlight – in moderate amounts – and that both kinds of light are extremely helpful for people with SAD.

11

While using light as an antidepressant is relatively new, heliotherapy – using sunlight to make ourselves feel better – is probably as old as humankind. Light has been used as a medicine for millennia. In the sixth century BC, Charaka, an Indian physician, treated a number of diseases with sunlight. Hippocrates and other ancient Greek physicians had their patients recuperate in roofless buildings, where they could soak up the rays of the sun.

Too much of a good thing?

The link between excessive exposure to the sun and various skin cancers is well known. In particular, sunburn – especially if you have a sensitive skin – has been highlighted as a risk factor for skin cancers. Australia, for example, has the highest rate of skin cancer in the world, long believed to be due to prolonged exposure to the sun.

Health education materials tell us to treat the sun with extreme respect, not to say fear. This is not new. A century ago, colonial Europeans were warned to wear protective 'solar topees' when going out in the African and Asian sun to avoid the dangers of intense sunlight. Sunstroke was an obvious problem, but these fears seem to have had a moral as much as a medical basis. Some doctors believed that the 'actinic rays' of the sun would sap the vitality of the European stock and lead to degeneration.

However, soaking up the hot sun for hours and hours year after year is different from getting more daylight in a northern hemisphere winter. Some influential health practitioners, such as Dr Jacob Liberman, believe strongly that the dangers of the sun have been greatly exaggerated. While too much strong sunlight (ultraviolet light) may be harmful, a certain amount is necessary to maintain life and health. UV light is said to lower blood pressure, make the heart more efficient, reduce levels of cholesterol, help weight loss and increase the levels of sex hormones. It also activates the skin hormone solitrol, which works with melatonin (see below). The exact health benefits of the sun are yet to be substantiated by controlled scientific studies, but few people would disagree with the idea that more time spent outside in our technological age can only benefit health.

Advice varies as to how much sunlight is healthy, but, in line with Dr Damien Downing's advice, the best way to get your sun is in moderation: 'in frequent, small doses, insufficient to burn you.'

What sunlight does to our bodies

Light is a key factor in balancing our brain chemicals and hormones so that we go to sleep and wake up appropriately.

When light enters the eyes, it hits the cells at the back of the retina (the rods). The nerve signals pass through the optic nerve to the visual cortex of the brain, so we can see objects. They also pass to the pineal gland, a pinenut-shaped gland within the hypothalamus that Descartes called 'the seat of the soul'. Among its many other functions, it controls the production of the hormone melatonin, a substance that promotes sleep and, according to some researchers, may even strengthen the immune system.

Your body stops producing melatonin when light reaches an intensity of 2,500 lux. While closing down the production of melatonin, light also boosts levels of serotonin, so making us feel more alert and awake. Towards the end of the day, as the sun goes down and the light disappears, melatonin release begins again with the move towards sleep.

These 'sleep/wake' and 'dark/light' rhythms are part of the body's 'circadian rhythm' – a 24-hour biological 'clock' that controls the timing of hormone production, body temperature and other functions as well as sleep. This clock is situated within the brain above the eyes, where a small cluster of brain cells (neurons) called the suprachiasmatic nucleus (SCN) receives information about the amount of light coming in through the eyes. The light informs the brain how active and alert we need to be, whether it is night and time to rest or day and time to work. Our internal biological clocks are synchronized to the light/dark cycle. In other words, although the body has natural daily rhythms, they are not completely automatic and rely on cues from light to back them up. The pineal gland seems to act as a kind of radar, scanning the environment to see how much light there is – the major environmental cue.

The pineal gland also influences other areas of the brain, such as the thymus, which is where the T-cells that fight infection are produced. So, sunlight is also implicated in the body's immune system and, indeed, a whole new area of sunlight therapy (based on medical work from the 1920s and 1930s) is emerging.

Sun and the body

Sunlight is said to produce a series of metabolic effects in the body that are similar to physical training. For example, tuberculosis patients treated with sunbathing are reported to have well-developed muscles with little or no fat, even though they have not exercised for months. Athletes routinely train in the sun, just as they did in ancient Greece.

Studies suggest that the heart works more efficiently after sunbathing, which increases the output of blood from the heart by around 29 per cent for five or six days after exposure to ultraviolet light. One study at Tulane University on the effect of sunlight on blood pressure showed that for men with normal blood pressure it had the effect of slightly lowering their blood pressure, which lasted for one or two days. For another group of men in this test who had high blood pressure, sunlight caused a greater reduction in their blood pressure and the effect lasted five or six days.

Conversely, lack of daylight seems to affect the heart adversely. Night shift workers suffer twice as much heart disease as the rest of us. In some workplaces, night shift workers are supplied with a pair of adjusting glasses or goggles to wear while returning home so that the daylight does not intrude too much into the retina of the eye, as this can be uncomfortable for them because they are used to the dark, but this does mean that they are exposed to very little daylight.

There is also evidence that sunlight lowers cholesterol levels. In one study, rabbits were fed a high-cholesterol diet. Half of the rabbits were placed in the sun, the others only experienced ordinary indoor lighting. At the end of the study, the sunned rabbits had clean arteries, while the others had severe accumulations and deposits of cholesterol in their arteries.

There is evidence that exposure to sunlight reduces the risk of developing internal cancers. Research studies in the USA and the former USSR have shown that breast cancer mortality declines with increasing sunlight intensity. An independent study of prostate cancer in the USA showed a similar result, as did a study in 1980 of colon cancer.

While there is much evidence linking sunlight and malignant melanoma, even this has been called into question. Some research has shown that continual exposure to daylight, as with people who work outdoors, actually reduces the risk of melanoma! Some studies find that 'intermittent' exposure, as in sunbathing, increases the risk; others do not. Obviously this does not mean that you should cast aside health warnings and rush out to stay in strong sunlight for hours on end. It is a confusing area and one where the 'crank' element can easily prevail. What does seem clear, however, is that our attitude to sunlight has been called into question, and that the healthy benefits of sunlight or just plain daylight should perhaps be remembered more often in our indoor age.

Certainly light is linked not just with psychological but with physical wellbeing at a profound level.

How it works

The explanation for the health benefits of sunlight seems to be quite simple. Vitamin D, a hormone, is made (synthesized) in the skin by ultraviolet light. Sunlight is the main source of vitamin D, although it exists in some foods. The role of vitamin D is multifacted and complex. Besides being essential for bone development, it helps the body absorb calcium.

The twentieth century saw the return of rickets in some areas. Incidentally, it was known as 'the English disease' because it was common in crowded smoggy cities in the UK. In the UK, osteoporosis, or fragile bones, affects three million women, with one in three at risk, and this also has been linked with vitamin D deficiency, especially among older people who may not go out as much and whose ability to synthesize vitamin D declines with age.

Lack of calcium has a number of effects on the body. While 99 per cent of the calcium in the body is used by the bones, the remaining 1 per cent is vital for:

- triggering muscle contractions, including those of the heart;
- nerve function;
- the activity of several enzymes;
- normal blood clotting.

The amount of calcium in the blood is controlled by several hormones, including vitamin D. Vitamin D carries the calcium to and from the bones. Lack of calcium is nearly always due to vitamin D deficiency (as the other cause is extensive surgery on the thyroid gland.)

Lack of vitamin D has been linked with SAD, and it is interesting

15

that joint pain is a symptom both of SAD and vitamin D deficiency. Supplementation, however, is probably not a good idea (see Chapter 10 for details). Vitamin D supplements have not been shown to help people with SAD, according to the small amount of research that has been done. It is definitely not wise to experiment yourself, as vitamin D supplements are toxic if taken in excess. While 400–800 IU daily is a relatively safe dose, vitamin D is not easily eliminated from the body. The body's own synthesis, on the other hand, is self-regulating.

It is much easier and safer (and cheaper) simply to get more daylight. Food sources of vitamin D include cod liver oil and oily fish, such as sardines, herring, mackerel, tuna, salmon and pilchard, while eggs, liver and butter provide a little. Food sources of calcium include dairy products, such as milk, yogurt and cheese, canned fish, if you eat the bones, hard water, dried figs, green vegetables, sesame seeds, bread and flour.

The effects of artificial light

Poor indoor lighting – or 'malillumination', to use a term coined by Dr John Ott – is an accepted feature of many people's indoor environments, yet it can have a drastic effect, creating symptoms of SAD.

Inadequate artificial lighting at work or school is so common that often we don't even notice it. Conventional fluorescent lights emit light that is deficient in many of the colours and wavelengths of natural sunlight. The usual indoor lighting, which makes use of incandescent bulbs, is mainly a warm, yellow or reddish light. Although this looks cosy, it is deficient in the blue end of the spectrum and contains virtually no ultraviolet light.

Numerous studies have shown the benefits of replacing ordinary fluorescent bulbs with full-spectrum ones as these imitate sunlight more closely. Health at work, health and behaviour in prisons, achievement and behaviour at school, all improve under full-spectrum lights, as has been shown in large, controlled studies. To list them all would take more space than is possible here, but let us look at a few. (See the Further reading section at the back of the book if you want to explore this subject more.)

16

The effects of SAD on children's performance at school, for example, have been demonstrated by long-term, large studies of schoolchildren. They show that children learn faster in classrooms with good levels of daylight than in darker or artificially lit rooms. One study of schools in Alberta, Canada, found that pupils improved greatly when given better light, especially in verbal creativity. Pupils working in rooms with the most natural light had learning rates improve by 26 per cent in reading and 20 per cent in maths.

In a study at the University of Illinois, sunlight treatments were given to half the members of a physical education class. The experiment ran for ten weeks and, at the end of the period, the group that was receiving ultraviolet light had increased their performance on a physical fitness test by almost 20 per cent whereas the other group had improved by just 1 per cent. The sunlight-enriched group also had half as many colds, their blood pressure went down and they showed a greater interest in their classwork than the sunlight-impoverished group.

Other studies have linked stress, anger and fatigue at work with the bright glare of fluorescent light, and have shown that natural light has a calming effect, leading to increased energy and productivity. Another study found that sales were 40 per cent higher in shops with skylights than in almost identical stores in the same chain that did not have skylights.

Access to natural light is one of the professional standards set for prison authorities. Having enough daylight reduces stress and promotes calm in both inmates and staff and has been shown to reduce levels of violence and further crime. Conversely, there has been concern about links between poor lighting and suicide rates in certain prisons. The first prime minister of India, Nehru, spent a lot of time in prison during India's struggle for independence. In his autobiography, there is one particularly striking passage where he recalls suffering from this lack of light in his tiny cell – his only source of light probably being a small kerosene lamp. The image sums up what many sufferers of SAD feel during their winter term of imprisonment. As the Victorian poet Emily Dickinson wrote:

> There's a certain slant of light,
> On winter afternoons
> That oppresses . . .

The effects of light deprivation

As mentioned, SAD is more common in countries in northern latitudes which have less light in winter. However, lack of light can creep up on us in many ways. People who work underground, such as miners, and those who work by night, such as nurses and other shift workers, are obvious examples of people deprived of daylight. But even people working in offices are at risk if the only time they spend in natural light is while walking the few steps from front door to car and car to entrance. Also, it's not just adults – look at how long the average child spends in a classroom.

Light deprivation can be subtle and may not always be realized. Your work environment influences how much light you get. Your offices might not have many windows, they may be small, or you might even just keep the blinds down all the time to prevent glare on your computer screen. In some workplaces, windows may be kept closed or darkened to save energy or the glass may be coated with light-absorbing substances. Computers themselves, increasingly used, may keep more people indoors – a factor to be considered with children and teenagers who routinely use the Internet to help with homework or as entertainment. Children also tend to spend more time indoors than past generations because the outside world is perceived as less child-friendly and more dangerous.

Another factor to be considered is modern trends in transport. We walk relatively little and use the car much more, which, again cuts down our exposure to daylight.

The following case histories illustrate how lack of light can cause SAD in people without their suspecting it.

Two years ago at the school where I work, an old room was converted into a modern IT suite, and I was put in charge. It had 22 new computers networked to other computers throughout the school and was the pride and joy of us all. So keen was I to get in there and start work that the last thing I noticed was that the room only had three tiny windows right at the top (previously the room, too small for ordinary teaching, had been used for storage).

The new suite was ready for use by the start of the academic year and, as we had a fine, sunny September and October, all went well. In November, however, I started to feel depressed, which I attributed to problems with a relationship.

18

By February I started feeling better. The next autumn, though, it was the same story, only worse. In that second year, it was a real struggle to come in to work. I really couldn't understand it. Here I was, with my own little kingdom, and I was desolate. Several times at break I would sit close to tears, without speaking to anyone. It all seemed too much and on two occasions I just walked out.

Obviously this could not continue. I was extremely lucky in that I had a sympathetic and informed headteacher who had been looking at research on the effects of artificial light on schoolchildren – as we frequently had to keep the blinds drawn because of the sunlight – and this was something that worried him. On the second occasion that I walked out, he had a long talk with me in which he mentioned SAD.

Once we realized what was going on, action was taken very quickly. I spent break, lunch and as much time as possible out in the open air. I also started light therapy in the mornings. A larger window was cut into one end of the room. My mood improved dramatically and I have never looked back. I can hardly believe that the utter misery I went through for two years was simply caused by lack of light.

Roy

Moving from a lighter to a darker house is another cause of depression that is often missed. It is a good idea to view prospective properties on a cloudy day, checking for factors like which direction the house faces for this reason. Janet's troubles began soon after she moved house.

I had a very pleasant, airy flat, but, as I loved gardening, I decided to move out of London to a house and commute in to my job as an admin assistant. I fell in love with a stone-walled cottage fronted by huge trees.

I loved it in the spring and spent a fantastic summer arranging the garden, inviting friends down for weekends and generally enjoying life. During autumn, I still spent a fair bit of time in the garden, but when winter came, for the first time I felt really down and lost all my usual energy. I wondered if I had made a mistake moving out of town and found myself making any excuse not to be at home – I'd stay with friends in town during the week or go home to my parents at weekends.

What I didn't realize was that I had bought an extremely dark, gloomy house. Not only was it north facing, but the trees opposite, which were evergreens, effectively blocked all the available light. The trees were privately owned and the owners refused to have them trimmed. The local council were unhelpful. I considered converting my attic and putting in lots of skylights, but, in the end, I reluctantly decided to sell. My first requirement for a new place was its light value. I asked the estate agents about window sizes before I even let them send me details.

Janet

The climate

Some people's sufferings begin when they move from warmer, southern climes to a more northern latitude with less daylight.

Marta was a Brazilian girl who came to the UK to study and work. She thought her seasonal depression only happened in people from sunny climates as they weren't designed to live in cloudier countries. She was surprised when she met Alison, the English girl whose story is told in Chapter 1.

Changes in weather may also affect some people. For example, even in summer, some find that a few dark, gloomy days or rainy days are enough to set them on the old path of depression. Conversely, in winter, a few fine days may be enough to lift their mood.

Glasses

John Ott – the researcher whose work has aroused interest in SAD – has described how his sunglasses and spectacles prevented sunlight reaching his eyes and that removing them resulted in a drastic improvement in his health. Previously he had been suffering from arthritis, frequent colds and respiratory infections. After breaking his spectacles and spending several days in the sun without them, he found his joints were much easier and looser, while a further week in the sun produced even higher levels of fitness.

So, it seems that even glasses can be a source of light deprivation as they may prevent light reaching the pineal gland via the retina. For those interested in finding out more about this subject, Jacob Liberman has written a book called *Take Off Your Glasses and See* (see the Further reading section at the back of this book). If you want to try spending time outside without your glasses, it's best to start at times when the sun is not too strong, such as up to mid-morning or after mid-afternoon. Never look directly at the sun, even in reduced light, to avoid damaging your eyes.

Another thing to bear in mind is that some people with SAD experience a manic phase in spring and so are sometimes recommended to wear dark glasses for part of the day, to calm down the too buoyant effects of the sun.

3

The symptoms of SAD

Is it really SAD or just the winter blues? How do you distinguish SAD from clinical depression? SAD brings a number of symptoms, some of which may be confused with 'ordinary' depression as well as with other disorders. According to the National Institute of Mental Health (NIMH) where pioneering work on SAD was done, and which has researched the subject for more than 20 years, one of the keys to diagnosing SAD is its regularity. It occurs during the same time of year, from autumn into winter.

So, the main factors that set SAD apart are:

- seasonal depression – starting and ending at a certain time of the year, usually autumn and spring – with feelings of hopelessness, guilt, misery, anxiety and sometimes suicidal thoughts;
- increased desire to sleep – oversleeping, difficulty waking up in the morning and daytime drowsiness;
- extreme fatigue and lethargy – lack of energy and motivation. Too tired to perform ordinary tasks;
- increased appetite and craving for simple carbohydrates and sweets, often leading to weight gain.

However, SAD can be as idiosyncratic as any other condition and may well include other symptoms, as you will see from the checklist and case histories below. SAD may also differ from year to year, with slightly different symptoms or with some years being more severe and others less so. According to the NIMH, while people with SAD may not experience severe symptoms every year, around seven out of ten winters are very difficult for them.

As well as overt SAD, there is a less severe, sub-clinical seasonal pattern known as the 'winter blues'. While many people experience the winter blues, Dr Norman Rosenthal, the person who named and defined SAD, worked extensively with the NIMH and is now the Clinical Professor of Psychiatry at Georgetown University, speaks of 'the grey zone' between the blues and SAD in which many people find themselves. According to Dr Rosenthal, many people who suffer from the winter blues mistakenly diagnose themselves as having SAD. They may just have less energy or be less productive or creative, without the sleep problems that characterize SAD. It is the point at which the condition becomes disabling that is the cause for concern.

If you do feel you may be suffering from depression, it is important that you consult your doctor as soon as possible as he or she can help. Look at the checklist below, which includes many signs of depression. In particular, symptoms may include negative thinking that is hard to shake off, difficulty in finishing tasks you previously found quite manageable, and persistent thoughts of death. SAD symptoms can mimic other serious medical conditions, such as thyroid problems or chronic fatigue, and these also need medical attention so it is wise to check with your doctor anyway.

Symptoms checklist

Many people experience some of the feelings and behaviours listed below at some time and many of these symptoms can indicate other forms of depression. Bear in mind that the first six in particular can indicate SAD.

Some research suggests that symptoms may become worse in the late afternoon as dusk falls, so this is something else to consider when monitoring your feelings.

- Depression that starts and stops suddenly at regular times of the year.
- Eating more than usual.
- Craving carbohydrates and sweets.
- Weight gain as a result of satisfying these cravings.
- Extreme tiredness.
- Sleeping more than usual.
- Lack of energy and loss of interest in activities.
- Sleep disturbance.
- Feelings of sadness and hopelessness.
- Cognitive problems – difficulty concentrating and making decisions. Tasks you previously found simple now seem complicated.
- Drinking more alcohol than usual.
- Drinking more coffee and tea than usual.

- Anxiety, tension and low tolerance of stress.
- Phobias.
- Irritability.
- Social withdrawal.
- Blaming others or circumstances.
- Wanting to stay at home, not go out.
- Loss of libido.
- Menstrual problems. Premenstrual tension may be worse than usual, with attendant irritability, sleep problems, appetite changes and low energy levels.
- Low body temperature.
- Minor physical ailments, such as increased sensitivity to pain, headaches, muscle and joint pain; digestive problems such as irritable bowel, constipation, diarrhoea; palpitations and night sweats.
- More prone to infections such as colds and flu.
- Keener sense of smell and changes in taste.

Symptoms in children and teenagers

Chapter 4 covers this in greater detail, but the list below is a useful starting point. The following are probably typical of all children at some time, especially towards the end of a hard week at school. However, if they are unusually pronounced or occur only in autumn or winter, they may indicate SAD. Symptoms to look out for include:

- irritability;
- bad behaviour;
- tantrums and crying;
- lowered performance at school;
- loss of interest in usual activities, especially sports;
- depression;
- not wanting to see friends;
- sleep problems at night and sleepiness by day;
- unusual craving for junk foods and sweets;
- reluctance to do jobs around the house that your child usually does not mind doing;
- headaches and other minor disorders.

Case histories

The following real-life experiences give an idea of how SAD can affect people.

Sally, a 41-year-old mother, felt that she just couldn't cope with the joint demands of her job and family.

> I had terrible mood swings and would feel very low and depressed. Also, I was very tired all the time – unnaturally tired. My memory was terrible – I'd go to the shops and forget what I went in for. I know everyone does this, but it was slowing my day right down. I got nothing done. I felt that I was being unfair to the children and ruining their lives and, at the same time I would be getting really snappy and irritated with them, screaming and shouting at them all the time – they seemed so badly behaved.
>
> When my husband came home from work, I would complain that the children went to him and didn't want me – of course they wanted him because they hadn't seen him all day. I was quite irrational. I remember standing in the kitchen thinking, 'If I go to my doctor and say I'm depressed, they may take the children away' and this seemed a very real possibility. I felt I was losing my mind.
>
> *Sally*

Marie, a 33-year-old lab technician, said she went into 'hibernation mode'.

> It's as if your whole system slows down. You don't want to go out, you don't want to have people round – just leave me alone. It's an effort to go to the shops and too much bother to have a bath sometimes – easier just to crawl back into bed. Sometimes I didn't even bother to get changed from my day clothes into pyjamas and would just spend days in the same clothes. The only thing I was interested in was sweets. I developed a passion for them, all kinds, and would spend ages deciding whether I was going to have chocolate or boiled sweets and where I was going to get them – very boring.
>
> *Marie*

Jon, a 39-year-old counsellor, suffered a range of 'horrible' symptoms.

A lot of them were physical – lots of aches and pains, to the point where I would be taking paracetamol all the time. I had digestive problems, including terrible wind! Night sweats were also a real problem – I'd wake up drenched. And total fatigue – I'd just want to lie down all the time. I had an absolute craving for sun and sunshine and always felt better if we took a winter holiday. I'd forget things all the time – PIN numbers, phone numbers. I lost interest in food and sex.
Jon

Atypically, Jon ate less and even lost weight in winter – around 2.7 or 3 kg (6 or 7 lbs). Unusually for a SAD sufferer also, he slept less and woke up very early – a classic symptom, in fact, of clinical depression. However, he knew he was suffering from SAD, first because it came on so suddenly – around the middle of September – and, second, because it was cured by light therapy. However, again, it is worth pointing out that SAD and clinical depression can overlap and can both be treated.

Both Sally and Jon said that they had suffered seasonal depression all their adult lives. Jon remembered having it in his twenties, while Sally recalled experiencing periods of depression as a child (SAD in children is discussed more fully in Chapter 4).

Depression

The depression is the key factor in SAD, with mood being so drastically changed as to affect most aspects of life. Feelings of sorrow or grief, a loss of self-esteem, hopelessness or even despair are all typical. Many people find it hard to work – the figures for time off work taken by SAD sufferers in winter goes up dramatically.

Depression can also show itself in different ways. For example, some people feel guilty, perhaps for their lack of energy or for overeating. Irritability is another symptom, sometimes leading to feelings of violence. As with clinical depression, you may feel you want to withdraw from the world and avoid social contact. These are feelings that we all may experience at times, but in SAD sufferers they may persist and affect many aspects of normal behaviour, including relationships.

Depression can also be masked as anxiety, panic, loss of confidence, paranoid thoughts. Poor memory and concentration are common. SAD can literally make a different person of you.

Barry was in his mid-20s and was admitted to the same hospital year after year, usually in late September and generally for several months at a time, so severe was his depression. Around February, he became better and was able to go home within a few days of this mysterious recovery.

The nurses first noticed that he became more sociable. Then he began to pay more attention to personal hygiene, changing his clothes and washing again. One day they heard music coming from his room and only then discovered that he had hidden his flute under his bed and was a talented musician. Through all the winters he had been hospitalized, no one had ever known he had a flute at all until that day! The nurses knew only the 'droopy' patient who would barely do a thing for himself, yet here was an energetic young musician who really seemed a completely different person.

Increased desire to sleep

The need for extra sleep can be disabling in severe cases of SAD. Sleep disturbance is a classic symptom of clinical depression, but, then, more usually manifests as early waking or inability to sleep. The urge to sleep longer is characteristic of SAD.

At the SAD clinic at the Royal South Hants Hospital, Southampton, UK, a study of 200 people showed that they needed two and a half to three hours more sleep at night in winter than in summer.

People may find themselves falling asleep earlier in the evening or have difficulty getting out of bed in the morning. Although people may be sleeping longer than usual, they may still feel tired or drowsy during the day.

I felt I could not get enough sleep. I resented being woken, no matter what the time, but didn't realize that I had already slept more than enough until my partner pointed it out to me. He became quite irritated at first, at having a hibernating bear

slumbering away all evening and all night. Then he became concerned, saying that ten hours a night was what a growing child needed, not an adult. In fact, it was the sleeping that first made me go to the doctor. My partner became worried that it was a sign of some illness, such as narcolepsy, and made me go. Needless to say I came back after various blood tests for anaemia and so on with a bill of clean health and not much the wiser – my GP thought I had 'maybe had a virus recently'.
Alison

Some people wake up during the night and sleep may be restless and less satisfying, so the fatigue can sometimes be a result of this. Equally, it may persist even when a person has slept a solid eight to ten hours, and some people may show signs of sleep-deprivation such as irritability and foggy thinking. These symptoms may be linked with low levels of brain chemicals. Current thinking on SAD points to brain chemical imbalance as a prime factor in the disorder (this is explained more fully in Chapter 4).

Extreme lethargy

One survey has shown that the extreme tiredness or lethargy they feel is what people find most disturbing about SAD. It may take different forms – inability to concentrate at work, loss of interest in your usual activities and a general lack of vitality.

It's just as if you were hibernating during the cold, dark months. I'd procrastinate about work and put as much as I could on hold. I couldn't make decisions. Facts would go round and round in my head and I lost the ability to organize them or to edit them. I was usually pretty good at binning junk mail and other rubbish the minute it hit my desk. With SAD, that ability seemed to go out of the window. I literally couldn't bring myself to look through all the reams of paper I seemed to receive – I just didn't have the energy. I kept my office door closed and my head bowed. Some days I'd just give up and go home. I felt 'too tired' the whole time, and close to tears. Some days I could have wept at work, and on a few I did. Those were generally the days I went home early.
Patrick

28

Increased appetite and weight gain

As if to combat the lack of energy, many people crave particular foods and may eat more than usual, sometimes bingeing. Indeed, SAD has been linked with eating disorders, such as bulimia and anorexia. The main foods people seem to crave are simple carbohydrates or starchy foods – pasta, white bread, cakes, biscuits, sweets.

The overeating can cause weight gain (typically from around 3–13.6kg/half a stone to 30lbs). In the study mentioned above at the SAD clinic at the Royal South Hants Hospital, 69 per cent of those taking part reported increased appetite, while 73 per cent craved high-energy foods. They reported a tendency to avoid salads and healthy foods, and all gained weight. Again, this is a normal occurrence during winter, but is not usually this extreme.

It is common to feel that you have no control over this excessive eating. It is believed that the urge to eat more simple carbohydrates may be a form of self-medication, an instinctive attempt to raise levels of the neurotransmitter (brain messenger chemical) serotonin, which influences mood. The way this works is explained more fully in Chapter 8, but it is useful to note here that this theory also explains why many patients respond favourably to selective serotonin reuptake inhibitors (SSRIs) and antidepressants such as Prozac or Zoloft.

In spring and summer, eating habits usually return to normal and people tend to lose the extra weight they have gained in winter – only to regain it the following winter. This cyclical problem is compounded by the fact that, sometimes, not all the weight is lost, with the result that some people end up overweight or even obese in the long term. The subject is tackled in Chapter 8 where we take a look at the theory that carbohydrate cravings are triggered by a lack of the brain chemical serotonin.

Comfort drinking

Some people find that they drink more coffee and/or alcohol during winter. The caffeine in coffee can be a powerful draw for people who are trying to combat the lethargy they feel. Some people may also drink more tea or soft drinks containing caffeine for this reason.

As caffeine dilates the pupils in the eyes, allowing in more light, which can boost serotonin production, increased coffee drinking can be seen as an instinctive attempt at self-medication for SAD. There is also evidence that coffee can mimic the effect of light in birds, according to work at St Elizabeth's Medical Center, Boston, and may help shut down melatonin production in humans. This is possibly another attempt by the body to treat itself.

Some symptoms as a result of excessive caffeine intake can mimic those of depression and may include indigestion, tummy pains, nervousness, panic attacks, palpitations and sleep problems.

Alcohol may also be used as a quick comfort. Because it provides the body with a simple sugar, it boosts certain brain chemicals and blood sugar levels temporarily, so raising sufferers' mood for a while. Again, alcohol cravings are thought to be a sign of decreased levels of serotonin. On the psychological side, for those who don't feel like taking their usual exercise, a spell down at the pub can also be an easy time-filler on a winter's night.

Too much alcohol can, of course, cause a wide range of symptoms, both physical and emotional, from headache to remorse. The long-term effects of consuming excessive quantities of alcohol are also well known and include damage to the liver, heart and brain cells. Alcohol is also a natural depressant, so once the immediate effects have worn off, the drinker with SAD tends to feel lower than before.

Seasonal mood swings

One feature of SAD is the way that your mood lifts in the spring. Many people feel an increase in energy and a dramatic lifting in mood. As if to make up for lost time, some throw themselves into work, tackling and completing projects with a surge of enthusiasm.

For some – though not all – people with SAD, this 'spring fever' can spill over into a manic phase (hypomania), which brings problems of its own. Ordinary judgement and the instinct for self-preservation seem to be blunted. Sufferers may find that they need far less sleep and rest and charge around expending energy without allowing adequate time to recharge their batteries. They may spend too much money and be generally impulsive, perhaps starting new relationships or jobs on the spur of the moment, upsetting old arrangements and disrupting relationships generally.

Although they have a lot of energy, it tends to be very unfocused. As they are easily distracted, they may have loads of ideas for projects and may start them but not finish any. A disregard for personal safety may spill over into aspects of daily life, such as driving, where greater recklessness brings an increased risk of accidents.

> I would have a difficult month in April. I would be speeding, in every aspect of my life. I'd walk faster, work more quickly, and talk faster too. My wife taped me talking during a manic phase. It was instructive! I literally talked much faster than normal and flitted about from subject to subject and woe betide anyone if they were to interrupt me. It was as if I had lost the ability to listen. I was also very argumentative, usually about trivial things. By May I would have calmed down.
> *Patrick*

As stated, 'spring fever' does not affect everyone. Some people simply resume normal productive life with feelings of relief while others have a stormier course through spring and may suffer ups and downs in line with the unpredictable weather.

Recognizing SAD

A classic symptom of depression is not realizing that you have it! SAD is no exception.

Steve, a 32-year-old banker, suffered several puzzling symptoms each winter and felt awful, but didn't know why. He lost interest in his usual activities, felt very tired and unmotivated, and was tearful and irritable, as well as experiencing sleep problems. He was much more emotionally sensitive than normal and felt he had less staying power to endure the trials of everyday life.

> I couldn't believe this was happening to me each winter. It went on for years until, one day, sitting in the office, I picked up a phrase on the Internet that led me to this article on SAD. It was a revelation. As I read, I could tick off almost word for word the list of symptoms. The article informed me that what I was feeling was the norm for SAD. I could have shouted with relief.
> *Steve*

Sally didn't realize just how depressed she was.

It's really difficult to see that it is depression when you're in the middle of it. I would have gone on like that if one day a friend hadn't come round. I told her I just wanted to walk out and leave them all. She said, 'This isn't like you.' She made me go to my doctor and came round and sat with the children while I went to the surgery. My doctor prescribed antidepressants, which were wonderful. She also suggested that we meet up in the mornings and get out to the park with our children. Now I know more about SAD, I understand that the daylight helps as much as getting out and having a break from the home routine.
Sally

Again, both these stories underline how important it is to go to your doctor or to talk to a friend you trust. Don't suffer in silence.

SAD and suicide

People tend to talk about seasonal depression in an ironic tone. It can be seen as a bit of a whimsical disorder. 'Does it really exist?' is the query from some who haven't encountered it. However, it is important to bear in mind that, in extreme cases, SAD is not only very real but can be life-threatening. As with other forms of depression, the risk of suicide should be taken seriously – the more so because it is preventable, with treatment.

At the Sleep Disorders Center in an American psychiatric hospital, a 35-year-old woman with SAD was admitted as an emergency patient after trying to commit suicide and nearly succeeding. The doctor who talked to her found out that she had SAD every winter, but was usually able to hang on until her children's school holiday in February when the family went to sunny Florida, which immediately lifted her spirits. This year, the February holiday hadn't come until the first week of March. She had been unable to bear it any longer.

SAD is treatable

Although awareness of SAD has been heightened over the past decade, many still live in darkness, both metaphorically and literally, with regard to this disorder. Millions of people who have varying degrees of SAD grit their teeth and just live through their symptoms for yet another winter, not realizing that, like other forms of depression, this is a treatable condition. The woman whose near tragic story is described above was successfully treated with bright light (this treatment is explained more fully in Chapter 7).

Many assume that they are simply not winter people and don't pursue treatment because they know their condition will improve with the arrival of spring. Why suffer, though, when you can do something about it? The remedies are covered in Chapters 5–10.

4
Serotonin and other factors

The latest research suggests that SAD is linked with an abnormality in the way serotonin functions. This brain chemical is a neurotransmitter (nerve messenger) in the hypothalamus, which is the part of the brain that controls mood, appetite, sleep and sex. Enough serotonin makes people feel calm, centred and balanced, while lack of it is a well-known factor in clinical depression.

In SAD, serotonin's role is implicated with that of melatonin – the hormone that induces sleep. It's a bit like a see-saw: too little serotonin results in too much melatonin, which is thought to be one reason for SAD sufferers' feelings of lethargy and lack of energy. The extra melatonin has primed the body for sleep – all day long. Overcoming SAD is believed to be a matter of getting this brain chemistry back in balance (Chapters 5–10 look at ways in which you can achieve this, including light therapy, diet and exercise).

Light deprivation is regarded as the main cause of SAD, but, with our increased understanding of the brain, it might be more accurate to call it the main trigger instead. While some people seem inherently more vulnerable to SAD – perhaps because of genetic factors – they may never develop it. Lack of light seems to be the factor that tips the vulnerable into actual depression. This can happen in various and sometimes unexpected ways, as we saw in Chapter 2 with the story of Janet who moved to a darker house and Roy who had to work in a room without natural light.

There are other theories as to what causes SAD. For example, there is speculation that it may be linked with abnormalities in bilirubin, a substance in the blood. However, at this time there is no way of making artificial bilirubin, so treatment using bilirubin remains only a possibility for the future. This chapter focuses on causes that can be dealt with, like serotonin. Bear in mind also that, as with any depression or mood disorder, life stresses may contribute, though, very often, sufferers agree that winter is the main trigger. Rachel voices a common finding:

Tasks that I sail through in the summer are so much harder,

sometimes impossible, in winter. In other words, my life can be going fine, but as the dull, dark days close in, every little thing seems too much.

Dr Rosenthal, who discovered SAD, believes that it may have more than one cause or else different causes in different people, with serotonin imbalances being responsible in some cases, melatonin in others and both in yet others. As with other depressions, individual variations have to be taken into account.

The serotonin factor

Interestingly, levels of serotonin are seasonal and are at their lowest in the winter. Good levels of serotonin are likely to make you feel balanced, optimistic and in control.

Serotonin, or 5HT, is a substance the levels of which can be raised by taking Prozac or a similar 'SSRI' drug. This neurotransmitter carries signals inside the brain, allowing the hypothalamus to 'speak' to the sleep/wake control area of the brain, the substantia nigra. If this communication process is impaired, then disturbances of mood and sleep tend to result.

Lower levels of serotonin, as well as making you feel depressed, may also make you feel scattered and unfocused in your thinking, unable to concentrate easily or with a short attention span. You may find work frustrating or be unable to complete a project that you know is well within your grasp.

Serotonin also influences impulse control, which enables you to refuse, for example, doughnuts, a creamy coffee or a glass of wine. Lack of serotonin, then, may lead to impulsive actions, such as eating a chocolate bar or flying into a rage simply because your brain is not giving you enough time to think decisions through before acting.

Research has linked low levels of serotonin not only with depression but with an increased craving for simple carbohydrates, such as pasta, bread, cakes or sweets. This craving is believed to be the brain's response to having low levels of serotonin – eating more starchy, sugary foods is an instinctive attempt to boost levels of serotonin in the brain. Unfortunately, the effect is only temporary.

Chapter 8 looks at how the right diet can boost serotonin levels naturally.

Research has linked exposure to bright light with the increased production of serotonin, Serotonin also influences the production of melatonin, which leads us on to the next part of the story.

Melatonin – nature's sedative

Melatonin is a hormone that helps control when we sleep and wake up. Identified in 1958, it has since been found to regulate many other hormones involved in controlling our circadian rhythm – that is, the 24-hour pattern of sleep and being awake.

Melatonin also controls the reproductive hormones in women, so affecting menstrual cycles and the menopause. Disturbances in melatonin production could be one reason for SAD being more common in women.

Children have the highest levels of melatonin. The levels drop with age, which perhaps explains why older people tend to sleep less or suffer sleep disturbances.

Melatonin also indirectly causes body temperature to drop, which may be another factor contributing to loss of energy and depression.

Like serotonin, levels of melatonin fluctuate with the seasons. During spring and summer, they are at their lowest as melatonin can only be produced in quantity during the relatively fewer hours of darkness. Conversely, the fewer the hours of daily light in winter, the longer is the period of time during which melatonin can be produced. Thus, it will have a stronger effect at this time of year, making you feel more lethargic in the winter months.

Normally, daytime levels of melatonin are very low and undetectable. Melatonin is excreted in high concentrations via the urine each morning, as shown in a study on morning auto-urine drinking (drinking your own morning urine is a traditional practice of yogic religion and is still widely performed to help achieve meditative states). In people with SAD who do this, daytime levels of melatonin tend to be higher.

Some research has also linked higher daytime levels of melatonin with an increase in the craving for carbohydrates. As carbohydrates create energy and raise body temperature, lowered melatonin levels could result in the need for more carbohydrates to help create more energy and body warmth.

Dopamine

This is another brain chemical that is present in the retina. Its production is stimulated by light and suppressed by melatonin. Again, abnormalities in response are thought to be linked with SAD.

Genetic factors

Is heredity a causal factor in SAD? It can be. Many SAD sufferers come from a family where a parent or close relative suffers from SAD. One study that looked at SAD in twins found that where one had it, about half of their twins also had the disorder. Other work has shown that there is a hereditary factor in at least 30 per cent of cases.

Researchers have discovered a gene that may make people more vulnerable to SAD. For a long time, it was suspected that SAD had a genetic component as it tends to run in families. Indeed, around 70 per cent of sufferers have one relative who has suffered from a major depression or other emotional or mental disorder.

The gene – known as 5-HTTLPR – is believed to affect the way a person responds to light, and was discovered by scientists at the National Institute of Mental Health, Bethseda, Maryland. It comes in short and long versions. The short version lacks some of the components that make up DNA – the material that contains the blueprint for the genes.

A study of 165 people showed that 75 per cent of people with SAD had at least one short copy of the gene. People with two short copies of the gene were much more likely to suffer from SAD than those with long versions. Of non-sufferers, about half had two copies of the long gene and half had two short copies or a long and a short copy. Another study of 200 people also showed that those with SAD were more likely to have a short version of the gene.

This does not mean that everyone with short copies of this gene will develop SAD. It may take an environmental factor to trigger it, such as an exceptionally bad winter or spending large amounts of time in a badly lit environment.

Another study at the University of Toronto found a link between a gene for tryptophan hydroxylase (an amino acid that is converted into serotonin) and SAD. Although the findings are preliminary, the study suggests that tryptophan – which would become serotonin in the body – might help people with SAD (see Chapter 10 regarding treatments).

Is SAD adaptive?

Animals either hibernate or are generally less active in winter, while at least nine out of ten people feel they eat and sleep more in winter. It is normal to have some seasonal response and mild hibernating behaviour is quite common. So, is part of SAD just a natural response to winter, a leftover state inherited from our ancestors to help us conserve energy?

Hibernation allows an animal to use the body's energy reserves at a slower than usual metabolical rate, so it is most active for the months of abundant food and good weather. Some ecologists refer to hibernation as 'time migration'.

There are differences between, for instance, bears and humans in winter. Bears have a drop in body temperature and appetite, whereas people with SAD tend to eat more. So, some have argued that SAD is a failure to adapt or else an adaptation process that has failed or stopped halfway. We retain some aspects of hibernation behaviours, such as sleeping more, but not others.

Life events and stress as triggers

Some psychologists do not view SAD as a disease, but as a social condition in people with stronger seasonal awareness than others who may suffer from the confines of society. According to this view, it is the demands of modern life that result in SAD, that we still have to get up and go to work or school when our primitive instinct would be just to laze around and eat.

Stress can trigger depression, be it classical depression or SAD. Some people have found that a stressful situation *plus* the onset of winter are enough to induce symptoms of SAD, though it is up to a doctor to determine exactly what type of depression it may be. In SAD, as in clinical depression, events that you might normally handle with ease seem just too much.

Many sufferers have found that SAD first developed after a stressful life crisis such as divorce, redundancy, bereavement or a new baby, that happened in winter. Someone who has previously shown only very mild symptoms may develop severe symptoms if put under stress.

Too much stress certainly does not help SAD sufferers and it may make sense to cut down on its sources.

Whom does SAD affect?

SAD can affect anyone. However, research suggests that certain groups of people may be more vulnerable to developing SAD than others. In particular, women are affected more than men, possibly because of hormonal factors, and women with PMS (premenstrual syndrome) seem to be a particular risk group. Research suggests that SAD may be related to other disorders, especially alcoholism, addiction, post-traumatic stress and eating disorders, such as anorexia and bulimia. However, SAD has also been reported in children.

As well as having *links* with other conditions, SAD can also be confused with other conditions, such as a viral illness or chronic fatigue. This is why it is important to get a doctor's opinion to make sure you are not suffering from another problem before you try the suggestions outlined in this book. Light therapy may not help with, for example, glandular fever. Bear in mind, too, that prolonged fatigue and depression may be symptoms of a wide range of conditions, from diabetes to anaemia. SAD may also be confused with allergic reactions or sleep disorders or with simple depression.

Women

Women are three times more likely to develop SAD than men. The reason for this sex difference isn't clear, but, according to Dr Rosenthal, it may be linked to female sex hormones. This theory is backed up by the fact that SAD decreases among post-menopausal women.

Premenstrual syndrome (PMS)

According to work by Dr Norman Rosenthal, at least half of all menstruating women with SAD have PMS, with symptoms ranging from irritability and sleep problems to bloating and depression. Some women experience PMS all year, but may be more severely affected in winter, while others may have PMS only in the winter.

Many women report similarities between the symptoms of SAD and PMS, such as depression, confusion, clumsiness, tiredness, craving for carbohydrates and weight gain. Some research suggests that serotonin levels drop dramatically in some women in the late-luteal (premenstrual) phase, causing these disruptive symptoms. However, the irritability and anger often reported in PMS is more typical of PMS than of SAD, where people are more likely to suffer from fatigue and lethargy. Also, disturbed sleep is more likely in PMS than SAD, where the need for more sleep is the norm.

Post-natal depression (PND)

There may be a link between SAD and PND. Certainly, women may be more at risk of depression after childbirth as they may stay in more and be exposed to less daylight, especially if they have their babies in the autumn and follow this pattern. Heather Simons, who has written SAD guidelines for the Cambridge-based organization Outside In (see the Useful addresses list at the back of the book), and has had SAD herself for more than 20 years, believes that many cases of PND are unrecognized SAD. 'Please, please try to have your babies in the spring!' is her advice.

Older people

Older people are at a greater risk of developing SAD because they may be less likely to go out into the light. SAD has also been linked with a condition prevalent in older people known as Sundowning or Sundowner's syndrome. This is commonly observed in care homes and is when some older people become more agitated or confused at the end of the day. Other symptoms include decreased attention, wandering and possibly also hallucinations and illusions. Both having visitors and light therapy improve this.

This condition has been described as the bane of young doctors who admit a confused older patient in the evening and wait to present them to a senior doctor in the morning, only to find the patient is perfectly well at that time of day! The minor neurological damage from which the person suffers is no problem after a good night's sleep.

Sundowner's syndrome often accompanies Alzheimer's disease. Other causes include illness such as pneumonia or heart attack, side-effects of drugs or any disease affecting the brain directly, such as stroke, seizures or a tumour.

The syndrome has been linked with SAD because it may also occur as a result of disturbances in the circadian rhythms – that is changes in the sleep–wake cycle, which is controlled by the pineal gland and, as mentioned earlier, such changes are thought to be implicated in SAD.

Sundowner's syndrome has been linked with so-called Hesperian depression (named after the Greek goddess of the dusk, Hesperus). This is when people show symptoms of SAD in the evening, once the sun goes down. For example, they may not be able to work or to go out once it is dark.

Children

Research suggests that many people with SAD have suffered since their childhood. According to a report in the *Journal of the American Academy of Child and Adolescent Psychiatry*, more than one million children in the US may be afflicted.

In a survey of children in a Minnesota school, 6 per cent said they experienced extreme mood variations during the winter, with 1 per cent reporting outright depression at that time of year. In another study of nearly 2,270 middle and highschool students in Washington, more than 3 per cent showed symptoms of SAD. The rate of SAD was found to be higher in teenage girls. The study concluded that between 1.7 per cent and 5.5 per cent of children between the ages of 9 and 19 may have SAD. It also speculated that there is a relationship between SAD and puberty.

SAD certainly seems to affect not just school performance but general development, including verbal creativity. A large study conducted in schools in Alberta, Canada, found pupils' performance improved greatly when in a classroom that got better light. Over two years, pupils in a classroom with full-spectrum light showed better results in achievement – also in rates of attendance as well as growth and development – than those in less well-lit classrooms. They even had better teeth, with fewer cavities!

How SAD presents itself in children

As many children – 2 to 6 per cent – have SAD as Attention Deficit Disorder (ADD). Even though the typical age for the onset of SAD is the late twenties, many children experience winter depression, often mistakenly labelled as laziness or learning disabilities. Many, with hindsight, recall their first episodes happening in childhood or adolescence. Children (and parents and teachers) may have difficulty recognizing SAD, especially given the lack of public recognition of this relatively new disorder.

SAD in children may take a slightly different form from SAD in adults. Children may be more likely to suffer from fatigue and irritability, or perhaps anxiety, rather than depression as such, though they may be more weepy than usual. They may also have sleep problems, including disturbed sleep, or the tendency to fall asleep during the day. Their increase in appetite may show as craving for junk foods or sweets. Some children also suffer headaches, perhaps because of the poor sleep and diet.

It is easy for both children and parents to miss all this. So much of this behaviour is regarded as 'normal' difficulties or teenage moodiness. What child doesn't want junk food or suffer sleep problems at times? Though children themselves may be aware that something is wrong, they tend to blame the problem on external factors, such as that a child or the teacher is picking on them or treating them unfairly.

Children may also show behavioural difficulties, such as withdrawal from family and friends, crying spells, temper tantrums and watching more television than usual without really retaining what they have been viewing.

When spring comes and the behaviour passes, it may be easy to label it as having been 'just a phase', to forget all about it and not to make the connection when there is trouble again at the start of autumn. So, it is worth monitoring symptoms to see if they are seasonal. Does your child behave differently on a winter holiday in the sun or snow? Bear in mind that white snow can reflect bright light, and so lift mood even though it may not seem sunny. Does your child's academic performance show any seasonal variations, with marks or levels typically going down in the autumn and winter? Does your child suddenly 'not want to go to choir or trampolining club any more' halfway through the autumn term? Does she bow out of going to the disco with her friends on a cold, dark Saturday night?

Other signs can be poor memory and organizational skills and difficulty in writing, finishing homework or completing projects. Again, these can also be indicative of a range of other problems, such as attention deficit disorder, and are also fairly typical of many normal children, so it is important not to jump to conclusions.

However, if SAD is the cause rather than something else, you will find that in spring, your child may well change, becoming more talkative and active, sometimes to the point of hyperactivity, and perhaps be unable to go to sleep early or find that they do not sleep well.

The cluster of symptoms – irritability, bad behaviour and sleepiness – often leads to children being disbelieved or wrongly labelled lazy or difficult. Undiagnosed SAD – and often it is not diagnosed at all – can make a child's life a misery and disrupt education, careers and relationships. Obviously, it is crucial to exclude other stresses, such as bullying or a feeling of being academically pressurized at school, as well as illness or other conditions. Attention deficit disorder may sometimes resemble SAD, as can clinical depression, but should not normally be more of a problem in autumn or winter unless your child has SAD as well. A visit to the doctor and a talk with your child's teachers should be arranged if you suspect your child may be suffering from SAD in order to find out for sure one way or the other.

People deprived of light

As explained in Chapter 1, SAD is more common in countries in northern latitudes as there is less light in winter in these parts of the world. However, people may also develop SAD-type symptoms in other seasons if they undergo a change in environment that involves them being exposed to less light than before. For example, moving to an area that is further away from the equator, and so has less sunlight, may trigger SAD in some people. Some people may be affected by a change in their environment or routine – moving into a home with less light or changing a work environment (for example, moving from a desk by a window to an indoor room without windows) or changing work hours so that they go to work by night. Climate can also have an effect, even when it isn't actually dark. Fog, for example, in coastal areas, can lead to SAD-like symptoms.

Others

Other groups of people have been shown to be more likely to suffer SAD than the rest of the population, though there are comparatively few studies on this. More research is needed to clarify exactly why some people seem to be more vulnerable.

People with eating disorders

One theory, as we saw earlier, is that serotonin plays an important role in both SAD and bulimia nervosa, and there may be a genetic reason for this. Both disorders are characterized by an increased food intake and depressed mood. One research project looked at three components of the serotonin system involved in satiety, production of serotonin and response to drugs that affect serotonin levels, such as Prozac, in women. It was found that women with SAD or bulimia nervosa were more likely to have a particular variation in a serotonin gene called tryptophan hydroxylase (TPH). SAD has also been linked with anorexia nervosa.

Research into this genetic link is in its early stages, but future studies could have a significant impact on treatment of both disorders, such as new medications targeting serotonin.

Alcohol and drug abuse

Those who use alcohol and drugs are two to three times more likely to develop SAD than those who don't, and it is believed that this, too, may be linked with an inherent lack of serotonin in the brain.

Several studies have linked alcohol cravings to lack of light. For example, one set of rats mysteriously preferred plain water during the week but went for alcohol at weekends. Researchers tracked this down to the fact that, owing to a fault in the timer switch controlling the laboratory lights, the rats were left in complete darkness all weekend. This finding was replicated and developed in other studies.

People prone to depression

People who suffer from depression may be more prone to developing SAD than people who have never suffered this. Again, this may be linked to serotonin levels.

Those whose culture demands they stay covered up
Apart from veils or masks, cultural expectations may also include staying indoors a lot of the time, which also cuts down on opportunities to be in the light.

People giving up smoking
Nicotine, like carbohydrates, increases serotonin, while nicotine withdrawal has the opposite effect. As we have seen, low serotonin levels have been linked with SAD.

People with eye problems
Partially sighted or blind people may suffer from SAD, but can benefit from natural light as it still reaches the retina. However, injuries to the eyes, certain eye conditions or loss of an eye may produce SAD, not just in winter but during more of the year, as less or no light is being received by the eyes.

Cataracts, for example, do not grow over the surface of the eye but they do cause narrowing of the lens, thus lessening the amount of light that can reach the retina. So, people with cataracts may be at increased risk of SAD.

People who wear dark glasses
Likewise, dark glasses and sunglasses can act as causes of SAD as they may block the light of rays from reaching the retina.

The benefits of protecting the eyes from UV rays have been well publicized, but in cases of SAD, there may be a case for taking the glasses off. However, care should still be exercised, keeping sunglasses on when the sun's rays are strong and only taking them off earlier or later in the day.

Is it SAD?

It is possible to have SAD *and* clinical depression or to have another disorder that may be confused with SAD or to have another disorder *and* SAD. To reiterate, it is worth checking with your doctor and getting a definite diagnosis before proceeding as if you have SAD.

Fatigue may be a symptom of almost any illness. Most usually, though, SAD can be confused with the following conditions.

- Classic clinical depression.
- Hypothyroidism (underactive thyroid), the symptoms of which are feeling sluggish and an intolerance of cold. The thyroid gland produces hormones that regulate the metabolism and abnormalities can be easily treated with medication.
- Hypoglycaemia (low blood sugar), which involves feeling weak, shaky and lightheaded, often with a craving for sweet things.
- Viral conditions as the symptoms of SAD can resemble those of glandular fever (mononucleosis, caused by the Epstein-Barr – E-B – virus), ME or chronic fatigue syndrome or post-viral syndrome. Viral conditions tend to be more prevalent anyway in the winter, so it can sometimes be confusing and difficult to diagnose the cause conclusively. A consistent history of depression experienced winter after winter may differentiate SAD from these other possibilities. Most viral conditions improve over time with rest and good diet and are a one off, so if the symptoms repeat from year to year, SAD should be considered.
- Sleep disorders, such as sleep apnoea (temporarily stopping breathing in your sleep).
- Allergic reactions. For example, pets as well as people spend more time inside the home during winter than other seasons, and an undetected allergy to cats or dogs can sometimes result. The symptoms of an allergy will result in poor sleep that, in turn, may be mistaken as SAD.
- Iron deficiency anaemia.

How is SAD diagnosed?

There is no one clinical test for SAD. It is diagnosed on the basis of your medical history, the main clue being whether or not it is seasonal.

Because the history is so important, you can help your doctor by keeping a diary of the symptoms. Points to note include:

- when the depression seems to threaten – some people start to feel apprehensive in August; others may be fine until late November or even December;
- changes in appetite – whether you eat more or differently;

46

- changes in sleep – in particular, whether or not you crave more sleep than usual;
- whether or not you have experienced any of these factors in previous years.

5

How to help yourself – an action plan

The prospect of the gloomy winter months creeping up on you again and again may make you feel powerless, but, there is action you can take to help prevent SAD or lessen its impact. Before you consider light or antidepressant therapy, outlined in later chapters, you may find that a few simple lifestyle modifications will help keep SAD at bay, especially in milder cases.

Taking into account that you may well feel more energetic and creative in spring and summer, it may be worth structuring your year consciously around this. Try doing major projects during the lighter days, and reserving the more routine tasks for the winter, instead of having the change of pace forced upon you. This gives you a greater sense of control and lessens any guilt involved in letting people down as autumn and winter approach and you feel you cannot honour commitments because it is too much for you.

In the same way, it may also be a good idea to postpone major life changes until spring. Many people do this instinctively, whether or not they have SAD. Moving house or starting a new job, for example, might be easier to manage in the spring, though this isn't always possible.

View autumn and winter as a chance to slow down and allow yourself to take life easier. Slip into a different rhythm from the busier days of spring and summer. Go to bed earlier and accept that you may not be as busy or as energetic as in the summer.

This chapter looks at ways in which you can try to pre-empt SAD and suggests action to take during the worst days of winter. It can also help if you try to establish some positive thinking about the seasons so that you can enjoy autumn and winter. For example, many people associate autumn with fresh starts and a surge of energy after the heat of summer – perhaps a remnant from schooldays when autumn means the start of a new year. Samhain is a celebration of the start of the Celtic new year at the end of October while Diwali is in November. Why not write down your ten best autumn and winter memories in a beautiful notebook to share with your friends and children? After all, if you have SAD, it may not be the seasons that are your enemy so much as lack of light, and this can be tackled.

Make the most of late summer

Use the last few weeks to top up on sunlight as much as possible. For most people this isn't a problem, but some begin to have feelings of impending doom and gloom in August as the light changes, becoming more mellow, with the shadows growing longer. Use these weeks to be outside as much as possible.

You can also use this time to plan for the autumn ahead. Start evaluating your levels and sources of stress and consider any ways in which they can be minimized. For example, if you have a difficult situation or colleague at work or foresee problems in a particular area, consult your superior while your energy and coping levels are still high. If you are at home with children, look at ways to make the daily school run easier. Try leaving a shoebox in the hall so shoes can't get lost and making packed lunches the night before.

You might also want to consider booking an appointment with your doctor for a general check-up or to talk about or make plans for overcoming winter depression. Your family doctor can be a source of support. Even if no medication is prescribed, it can be helpful to know that you have discussed the possibility with him or her. Your doctor may also be able to refer you to a psychiatrist and, as the appointment may take time to come through, late summer is a good time to start the process off. Points to discuss can include general goals and whether or not to start light treatment using a dawn simulator or lightbox and if drug treatment would be appropriate.

You could also research alternative therapists in the area (see Chapter 10) and speak to two or three over the phone. Enter their names, numbers and your reactions in your address book and have these details ready in case you feel you may need them in the future.

Plan autumn activities

Having said this, some people find it helpful to have regular events to attend. September sees the start of a whole new batch of day and evening classes, so late summer is the time to consider taking up something to ensure you are occupied and so less likely to fall prey to depression. While many people with winter depression withdraw and don't feel like socializing, company in a structured environment, such as a class, can be less demanding. This is because you can be working away at your woodwork, creative writing or whatever without feeling obliged to talk all the time.

Another option is a group activity, such as singing. The run up to Christmas is a busy time for most choirs and singing has proven health benefits of many kinds. One large Swedish study of more than 12,675 people found that singing in a choir seems to promote longevity as well as boosting health and mood.

The value of planning is that it helps you feel more in control. Plan something for each weekend of the month. 'Having something to work towards, like cut-price cinema or concert tickets, is one of the best ways of raising wellbeing and efficiency', says occupational psychologist Cary Cooper.

Plan treats and make the most of the Christmas entertainment season. Feeling isolated can be a dangerous aspect of depression. It is hard to bear in mind that changes in brain chemicals may be responsible for this feeling rather than social reality. Arranging regular company can combat this. Get together with another friend who hates winter to encourage each other to go out, stick to an exercise plan or contact other SAD sufferers (see the Useful addresses section at the back of the book).

Into winter – planning your routine

Many people find mundane chores such as cooking and cleaning more of an effort in the winter, so plan ways to save yourself energy.

- Do your major food shopping on the Internet. Some people find that doing this once a fortnight or with a friend splits any delivery charges into manageable size.
- Consider investing in having someone help with cleaning or ironing – even once or twice a week needn't cost too much and may make all the difference to your level of coping.
- Cook several meals in advance at weekends when you have more time, or in early autumn when you feel more energetic. For example, bolognese sauce can be frozen in separate portions to serve for a pasta meal, shepherd's pie or curry.

- Buy any items for your winter wardrobe when they first appear in the shops in early autumn before you get too lethargic to bother, making sure you have enough warm socks, tights and other items. Many SAD sufferers feel better for being extra warm (see Keeping warm on p. 55).
- Invest in extra help with childcare.

Planning for Christmas

Christmas can be a stressful event at the best of times, but if you have SAD, you may well find it overwhelming. There are several options. One is not to bother with Christmas at all. Indeed, Mary and her family, who were Quakers, didn't celebrate Christmas with presents, cards and festive meals.

> We made a decision early on in our marriage simply not to 'do' Christmas. The children have never known any different and I don't think they quite know what people are going on about when the Christmas fuss starts.
>
> I do find managing daily life hard enough in the depths of winter anyway and Christmas seems so complicated! People send us cards, which is quite nice, though I always feel a bit guilty, but then I think, 'Oh well, I can make it up to those people all the rest of the year round.' And in a week or so's time everyone's forgotten about it all anyway, so it makes no difference. It is a peculiar time bubble.
> *Mary*

Another option is to prepare for the event while your energy levels are still high – in late summer if it suits you. Some people buy presents all the year round as and when they see them, so it may be worth clearing a drawer or shelf especially for Christmas and putting bargains away there. Another idea is to shop online or by catalogue from late summer on. Jane finds this approach helpful. And it is a time of year when she saves herself from as much stress as possible.

> I've learned to buy cards the minute they appear in the shops – this seems to be earlier each year, which in a way is quite good for someone with SAD! I even buy the stamps and put them on,

then put the whole lot away to be posted in December. I used to write a short letter of news and print out a copy to put into each card, as any real news I would probably give over the phone. Over the past couple of years, though, I've dropped this and just copied a short e-mail to everyone.

I buy frozen Brussels sprouts, I don't invite hordes of draining relatives, and we tend to go out to a hotel. I'd love to go to Paris but haven't felt up to it yet.

Jane

Monitor your moods

Instead of just waiting for your spirits to sink at the end of summer, try to take pre-emptive action. Remaining conscious of your moods means you can stay a step ahead of them instead of being totally at their mercy.

One idea is to keep a diary or mood chart, listing your moods and any factors that seem to trigger them. For example, a grey morning may leave you feeling down, especially if you have overslept, realize you have forgotten to get any cash out, received only a bill in the post and have to rush off to work.

Ensuring you have a quiet five minutes for meditation or to sort out your thoughts can help, as can writing positive affirmations, such as 'I can manage, whatever the circumstances.'

Keep an eye open for the symptoms of depression. A frequent comment from people with depression is that they find themselves in the middle of it without seeing it coming. You might want to make your own checklist, as people can have different warning signs from each other, or ask your partner or friend to let you know when they notice changes. Often others are better at seeing that something is not quite right than we are.

Signs that can indicate depression include:

- undue pessimism;
- lack of motivation;
- low self-esteem;
- withdrawal from others and feeling isolated;
- feeling guilty;
- feeling irritable;

- feeling overwhelmed and unable to cope.

I certainly don't always realize that I'm 'going down'. I am aware of being grouchy and blaming everyone around me for everything, but I'm not really aware of how negative I am until others challenge it – and it can take a bold person! One morning I'd run down the entire British system, from education to the trains and postal service, and after a short pause my partner said, 'Anything good to say about anything?' That made us both laugh and I realized how irrational my thinking had become.
Alison

Monitor your energy levels

In the same way, keep an eye on how energetic you are feeling. When your energy seems to start trailing off, you can steer a path between trying to raise energy levels and adapting to a quieter lifestyle.

Ways to raise energy levels include:

- diet (see Chapter 8);
- exercise (see Chapter 9);
- light therapy (see Chapter 7);
- exposure to more daylight (see this chapter and Chapter 2).

As before, keep a diary – this time for planning the months to come. Consider invitations before accepting them. Ask if you can ring people back in a few hours' time and use that time to think through whether or not you can comfortably manage what is involved or not. An autumn weekend with friends, running a stall at the school Christmas fête, a work Christmas party – all these things may take up energy that, at that time of year, you feel you want to keep for other activities. There is no harm in saying no, either in advance or later on, if you do feel you have over-committed yourself. You can always undertake new projects or honour social obligations in spring or summer instead.

Organizing your memory

Poor memory can be a particular problem for some people with SAD. Try to find one simple way to organize your diary. Having a large wallchart may help or an electronic personal organizer.

Katy kept an organizer on her at all times and would immediately enter anything into it as it crossed her mind, even walking down the street. She found that if she wrote things down she was 98 per cent certain to accomplish them. This system broke down, however, when the battery ran out as she kept forgetting to buy a replacement!

Mary keeps a small diary with birthdays, appointments and so on written in it, which has the bonus of not relying on batteries.

Jayne uses an index box with small cards on which she's written names and addresses. She found it hard to remember to use a diary or organizer, whereas the index box sits on her desk so she can use it as she works.

Getting more natural light

Even in winter or on dark days, or in shade in summer, you can enjoy the health-giving qualities of sunlight by getting outside for as little as 20 minutes a day. Here are some ideas to help you.

- Aim to spend at least an hour a day outside, whatever the weather, breaking the time up into smaller portions if this is more convenient than going out for the whole hour in one go.
- If you wear glasses, remove them, if you can, for at least 20 minutes (longer if possible) as they can block the entry of sunlight to the eyes and slow down its effects on the body.
- If you cannot get out, spend some time sitting by an open window. The window needs to be open as glass absorbs UV light, denying you of these beneficial rays that activate vitamin D.
- Some research has suggested that certain suntan lotions may be linked with cancer. According to the US Food and Drug Administration, 14 out of 17 lotions contain suspected carcinogens in the form of PABA (para-aminobenzoic acid). However, some authorities believe PABA allergy to be more of an issue than the risk of cancer from this substance. To be on the safe side, use a PABA-free or chemical-free lotion. Depending on what type of skin you have, try also allowing yourself some time in the sun without suntan lotion. You can wear a long-sleeved top and so on to protect your skin.
- Never look directly at the sun.
- Avoid exposure when the sun is at its strongest – usually between 11 a.m. and 2 p.m.

Lighten up your home and work

Decorate your home to make the most of light and bright colours that reflect the light. Fit daylight bulbs that create full-spectrum light (see Useful addresses). Open curtains and blinds to let natural light into the house and prune any trees or hedges that cut out your natural daylight. You could also consider putting extra skylights and windows in your home.

At work, try to sit near a window or at least ensure that the lighting is adequate. If necessary, bring your own in, preferably fitted with a daylight bulb.

Keeping warm

Many people with SAD (and without!) report feeling better if they keep warm, so late summer could be a time to overhaul your house and plan for efficient winter heating. If there are any problems, you will feel far more like dealing with them than in winter.

- Check the roof insulation and, next time it rains, test that no broken tiles are letting any moisture in.
- Run the heating to make sure it works and bleed radiators of any excess air as this makes them less efficient.
- Consider fitting extra radiators in cold corners or rooms you don't normally use, such as a conservatory or loft, to extend liveable areas and make the house generally warmer.
- Order in logs and coal if you have an open fire – prices are sometimes cheaper before the autumn season starts.
- Consider having double glazing fitted in some rooms (it keeps out noise, too). If this is not an option for you there are other ways to insulate windows – ask your local DIY shop for ideas.
- Don't skimp on heating. If you don't want to heat the whole house, invest in extra heating for the room you spend most time in.
- Some people enjoy an electric blanket, but some research has linked prolonged use of them with cancer, especially leukaemia. It is believed that they lessen the production of melatonin, which fights cancer. However, new blankets, which use more modern methods of wiring, may be less risky. If you are concerned,

preheat the bed, then switch the blanket off when you are ready to sleep. A traditional hot water bottle is another option.

Sleep well, but less

Craving for sleep has been mentioned as a symptom of SAD, but it may help not to give in to it all the time. While a good night's sleep is essential to a balanced mood, research shows that sometimes restricting excessive sleep can help boost your mood and energy levels. Save lie-ins for one day a week, and try to get up at a reasonable hour each morning. You may find this easier if you use an alarm clock that works by faking a dawn (more on the benefits of this in Chapter 7).

It may also help to go to bed at roughly the same time each night as this is more likely to set your biological clock and lessen the possibility of disturbances to sleep – a factor linked with SAD.

Some people may benefit from having a siesta. Research by the Sleep Council has found that 38 per cent of us work best in the morning, 41 per cent of us in the evening, showing that we have a natural inclination to snooze at midday.

It will be easier to have a good night's sleep if you don't exercise, work, eat a large meal or drink alcohol before bedtime. Reading by low light and having a glass of warm milk may help soothe you off to sleep. Sex and chocolate also work well, according to research by the Sleep Council!

Keep physically active

Ideally, of course, physical activity should be a year-long part of your life, not something reserved for specific times. However, assess your level of physical activity in late summer and see what you can do to keep busy as the darker days come along. For example, even gloomy days often seem less overpowering if you are out, so walking to the shops or to work could be an option.

Get outside

Wrap up warm and go for a walk in the park for 20 to 30 minutes to raise your serotonin levels. Surprisingly, even a cloudy winter's day in the UK provides 10,000 lux of natural light.

The light striking the retina activates the pineal gland, which, in turn, controls production of the energizing hormone serotonin.

If you wear glasses, take them off outside for at least 20 minutes a day, as they can block UV rays and stop them reaching your retina so you lose out on a boost to your serotonin level.

When you are at work, get outside at lunchtime. Generally make the most of any opportunity to be outside.

Consider taking a winter holiday

Many people with SAD instinctively plan a holiday in the sun when their spirits are likely to be at their lowest ebb, usually around January or February.

Ideally we would be away from December to February. We'd also love to go away for Christmas but it's too expensive. Prices seem to drop in January, so we go then. We just take a cheap package to the Canaries and soak up the sun for two weeks. It's not quite enough to get us through to the very late springs we've been having – but it helps. If spring came when it ought to in February or March, we'd be okay – but we've been having to wait until April for the leaves to appear.
Sally

Relocating

Moving to a sunnier country may sound extreme, but if you find life a misery for half the year, it at least deserves to be considered. You do need to think carefully about whether or not the benefits of extra sun will be outweighed by the changes in major life factors, such as your job, family, friends and culture. First, spend some time assessing how well SAD can be controlled by other means, such as light therapy and warmth, if your needs would not be met by a sunnier location.

If you decide to go ahead, still take care. Pay several visits to the place in winter to ensure you really will feel better there – if possible for longer than the usual two weeks. Be sure to check the weather conditions right through the winter. This is because south does not always mean sunny – witness the mistral in southern areas of France.

Also, check that summer doesn't mean more heat or humidity than you can stand as this can not only be uncomfortable but also, in some cases, actually trigger summer SAD (see Chapter 1). This is when, contrary to most seasonal depression, people feel depressed during the summer.

Seek help if need be

Make the most of days when you feel better. We all have daily fluctuations in energy, so remind yourself that if you feel low one day, you may be more able to cope the next.

If, despite your best efforts, you find you cannot manage and that your mood and wellbeing are sinking, do seek support.

6

Healing light – a history

In 1905 Einstein put forward his theory of relativity and postulated that light and matter are interchangeable: 'Light is not just a pleasant side-effect of summer; the whole world runs on light energy.'

His words came in the middle of an era when interest in the healing value of light was at its height, not just for depression and other psychological ills, but for a host of physical illnesses as well. In 1877 it was discovered that sunlight killed off the bacteria of diseases, including tuberculosis, cholera and anthrax. In those days, TB was 'the captain of the armies of death'. Today, anthrax, with the threat of its use in biological warfare, may hold the most immediate terror, but the return of TB in some areas is also a cause for concern.

Over the next 30 years, further scientific research pinpointed UV rays as the 'active' part of sunlight's therapeutic effect. In 1903, the Danish doctor Niels Finsen was awarded the Nobel Prize for showing that ultraviolet rays were effective against tuberculosis. Sanatoria to treat tubercular patients by sunlight were set up, such as that of Dr Auguste Rollier in the 1920s and 1930s high up in the Swiss Alps. Both children and adults were taken out into the sun during the day for precise periods of exposure, starting with just five minutes at a time, and many hospitals (unlike hospitals today) were designed with verandas and French windows to make this easier.

Sunlight or UV therapy became widely used for treating many other conditions, such as wounds, which healed more quickly and with less scarring in the sun. Sunlight was (and is) also believed to be helpful for osteoporosis and the immune system, among its many other benefits. Sunlight was generally seen as good for both physical and psychological health – including depression and lethargy – and the cult of sunbathing began during these years.

The arrival of penicillin wiped out not just bacteria but interest in the medical value of sunlight. Penicillin – so much more dramatic and immediate in its effects and needed urgently in time of war – heralded the start of the drugs era. From then on, the drug industry grew rapidly, along with the concept of the instant medical fix and a pill for everything. There were few financial rewards in the relatively time-consuming pursuit of light as a treatment for illness when drugs could do the same thing in less time much more cheaply and it has taken until recently for interest in the therapeutic value of light to revive. Light therapy for SAD only appeared in the 1980s. However, interest in the healing sun goes back much further than this.

Heliotherapy in the past

Heliotherapy, or sunlight therapy, probably dates from when primitive man, deeply depressed by yet another chilly night in his cave, emerged each morning to extend his stiff, cold limbs to feel the sun's healing warmth. In the sixth century BC, Charaka, an Indian physician, treated a number of diseases with sunlight. Native Americans traditionally use the power of natural elements, including sunlight, in age-old healing rituals. Many other ancient 'solar cultures' made use of solariums to stimulate and maximize physical and mental wellbeing, including the Romans, Incas, Aztecs, Egyptians and the Greeks.

The word 'helios' is Greek and means sun. The ancient Greeks made regular use of sunlight for health purposes, practising 'arenation' or 'heliiosis' – baring the body to sunlight in 'aerinaries', which were roofless buildings.

Hippocrates and Pythagoras wrote extensively on the use of sunlight in the processes of healing, while Herodotus is known as the father of heliotherapy because of his firm belief in the healing properties of the sun. He made regular use of the sun in his own medical practice. 'Exposure to the sun is highly necessary for persons whose health is in need of restoring,' he wrote. 'In every season, the patient should permit the rays of the sun to strike full upon him.'

Then as now, however, exposure was to be judicious. 'But, especially in the summer, this method should be lessened because of the heat', adds Herodotus.

This balanced statement perhaps represents what we should be aiming for today. Sunlight therapy is an area where the excesses can be viewed as a threat. On the one hand, there is a growing body of scientific opinion, that purports that the benefits of sunlight to health are being overlooked, while, on the other, is a well-established body of opinion that views UV rays as harmful and the sun a danger. This is reflected in light treatment for SAD, where UV rays are routinely screened out of lightboxes.

Another Greek doctor who wrote about sun therapy was Antyllus: 'Persons expose themselves to the sun, some cover themselves with oil and others do not; some lie down, resting on sand or a cushion, and some are seated, while others stand or play. This sunlight exposure prevents an increase in body weight and strengthens the muscles. It makes fat disappear. It also reduces hydropic swelling.'

These ideas are still under discussion today. There is a wealth of literature on the effects of sunlight on the prowess of athletes and whether or not muscle growth can be speeded up by sunbathing (Chapter 2 looks at modern research on the health benefits claimed for sunlight).

Sun worship

The world was said to begin with the command, 'Let there be light', and there are 200 references to light in the Bible. In modern Christianity and in much New Age philosophy, light is a metaphor for the sublime. This is a remnant of the cruder sun worship, which prevailed in many cultures from earliest times. Focusing on the power of the sun and often linking reverance for this with magic, rather than religion, occurred very frequently too.

The ancient Egyptians worshipped the sun god, Ra, represented by a golden disc, which was also a symbol for the king. The god Apollo represented the sun for the Greeks. The Mayans in South America were renowned for sun worship, building huge pyramids in Mexico. The Incas, from AD 1200 until the sixteenth century, worshipped the sun god Inti and his wife Kilya, the moon.

In Europe, with its mainly Judaeo-Christian traditions, the early Christian church found it much easier to make use of existing traditions – rather than sweep them away and start again – in order to ensure that its beliefs would be accepted. As James Frazer documents in *The Golden Bough*, the Christmas festival of light is superimposed directly on to older pagan celebrations of the re-emerging sun, especially for the old Persian deity of Mithra, who was directly identified as the sun by his worshippers.

The whole idea of a newborn infant at Christmas goes back much earlier than Christian times. The day of the winter solstice was seen as the nativity of the sun, as the hours of daylight begin to lengthen from 25 December. The Egyptians, among others, used a baby to represent the newborn sun. 'The ritual of the nativity, as it appears to have been celebrated in Syria and Egypt, was remarkable,' comments Frazer. 'The celebrants retired into certain inner shrines, from which, at midnight, they issued with a loud cry, "The Virgin has brought forth! The light is waxing!"'

In ancient Britain, too, worship of the sun became part of early civilization. The stones of Stonehenge, built on Salisbury Plain between around 2000 and 1500 BC, are aligned to indicate the solstices and the beginning of seasons, the coming of light, and to predict eclipses of the sun and moon.

The decline of the sun did not pass unmarked by ancient peoples either. The summer solstice was celebrated by festivals all over Europe from Ireland to Russia. The midsummer fire festivals – marked by huge bonfires, animal sacrifice and dancing – were the most important of the year among the primitive Aryans of Europe, as they marked the time of year when the sun begins its decline. 'Such a moment could not but be regarded with anxiety by primitive man', remarks Frazer, and perhaps our collective memory has inherited some of this angst today. Could it be that inherited racial anxiety about the declining sun constitutes a biological basis for SAD?

Research into light

In 1666, Isaac Newton made the startling discovery that white sunlight was composed of the seven colours of the rainbow when a prism was used to filter it. Thomas Edison changed night and day for good when he invented the incandescent light bulb in 1879. In many ways, we have progressed remarkably slowly since then. So overpowering has been the utilitarian use of light – to extend the day and productivity – that more diverse and creative forms of lighting, such as lighting devices for therapy, have only been developed in recent years.

The influence of light and dark on biological rhythms was first described in 1729 by the French astronomer Jean-Jacques de Mairan.

His work with the small red flowers of the plant *Kalanchoe blossfeldiana* proved that even plants follow circadian rhythms if they are to flourish. The 1900s saw burgeoning scientific interest in the effects of various colours on plants, animals and people. Many of the studies took place in the US where, in 1876, Augustus Pleasanton used blue light to relax glands, the nervous system and the organs. In 1887, Seth Pancoast used red and blue lights to stimulate and relax the nervous system. In 1878, Dr Edwin Babbitt developed the chromodisc for filtering light on to the body and also pioneered the use of charging water placed in glasses of different colours with sunlight as 'solar elixirs'.

In the 1920s, Royal R. Rife developed the Rife Beam Ray, designed to destroy bacteria or viruses and diseases, including cancer. In 1934, his work curing cancer achieved a success rate of more than 90 per cent at the University of California. In the 1920s Dinshah Ghadiali developed a machine that beams light of different colours on to different parts of the body – the spectrochrome.

Dr Harry Riley Spitler of the College of Syntonic Optometry developed the use of coloured light, delivered into the eyes, to improve vision, balance the nervous system and achieve other benefits.

More recent pioneers

The growing interest in sunlight and light therapy in our time can be traced back to several pioneers in the US and Europe who kept going during the years when official medical interest was at its lowest.

John Ott, a Chicago banker, became interested in the impact of light on the growth of plants in 1927 after noting that a pumpkin produced all-male or all-female flowers depending on which type of light it received. Ott went on to research the impact of light on animals. He also founded the Environmental Health and Light Institute and designed indoor lighting that mimicks natural light. His work is at the core of much of today's research into SAD.

Dr Jacob Liberman believes that the dangers of UV rays have been greatly exaggerated and that we are depriving ourselves of their health benefits by hiding behind windows, sunglasses and suntan creams (and there have been concerns about the latter being carcinogenic). His book *Light: Medicine of the Future* (see the Further reading section at the back of the book) is a pioneering work on the health-giving value of sunlight and the need for proper artificial lighting.

The discovery of SAD

Research leading to the definition of SAD began in the US in 1970 when research engineer Herb Kern noticed regular changes in himself during the winter months. Happy and productive in spring and summer, every winter he would become depressed, lethargic and have problems with his work.

Kern developed a theory that his mood and energy levels were related to the changes in levels of light at different times of the year and he approached scientists working on bodily rhythms at the National Institute of Mental Health at Bethseda, Maryland, who improvised a lightbox. Within a few days of this lightbox treatment, Kern's symptoms improved noticeably.

Encouraged, the scientists tried more experiments. Each experiment resulted in people finding that, with light treatment, their symptoms lessened or even ceased completely. The discovery of SAD had been made – at the same time as its cure.

SAD was first described and named nearly a decade later by Norman Rosenthal and his colleagues at the NIMH. Rosenthal researched the links between abnormalities in the body's biological clock and depression, and the effects of light on the brain and body.

Rosenthal, a doctor from South Africa, came to study and work in the United States. He, like Kern, noticed that his mood and behaviour changed during the winter months. His energy levels dropped dramatically, he was filled with foreboding and anxiety and depression ruled. In spring, his energy and mood soared once more.

Now renowned for his work on the seasons, Dr Rosenthal eventually traced his own depression to the lack of light during North American winters after working with other scientists at the NIMH who had discovered that bright light could stop the production of melatonin at night.

Drawing parallels to the natural seasonal changes in animal behaviour and biology, such as hibernation, Rosenthal speculated that depression in winter may be due to human beings' inclination to hibernate: 'Perhaps we are closer biologically to our animal brethren than we first thought.'

In the decades since then, there has been an explosion of interest in the condition and increasing research into it, though far more is needed to gain a proper understanding of SAD.

As this chapter has shown, SAD has not sprung into society out of the blue. Our need for light is deeply rooted in our biology and our history.

7
Light therapy

Because it isn't always possible to hop on a plane to a sunnier land, phototherapy, or light therapy, is the leading treatment for winter depression. It has a high success rate – around 85 per cent of people find it helpful. SAD expert Professor Chris Thompson of the Royal South Hants Hospital, Southampton, UK, has found that people are three times more likely to get better if they receive more light than if they receive less. Colour blind (and blind) people respond just as well. Light therapy may also avoid the need for drugs and it has minimal side-effects. It does involve some initial expense and it can be slightly time-consuming. However, the expense is fairly low while modern light treatments are becoming more sophisticated and it may only be necessary to have two sessions of 20 to 30 minutes a day. The benefits of being free of depression far outweigh these minor disadvantages for most people.

It is possible to buy and use light therapy devices yourself and they are much more readily available now than even a few years ago (see the Useful addresses section at the back of the book). It is recommended that you consult your doctor before using one, though you may find that some GPs do not know that much about light therapy. Light treatment is considered to be relatively safe, but you may benefit more with proper guidance, although many people can and do use the equipment by themselves.

What is probably more important is how severe the depression is. If you experience serious depression, feelings of 'life not being worth living' or you cannot complete tasks that are usually not a problem, then you should consult your doctor as soon as possible. Those with eye problems should also get medical advice before using light treatment.

Indoor sunshine

There is a long history of the use of 'indoor sunshine'. By the 1890s, European sanatoria were prescribing incandescent electric 'light baths' to treat many physical and psychological conditions. The subject of growing research interest since the early 1980s, light therapy is now widely used, in spite of some scepticism from the medical establishment about a syndrome very few have ever seen as only an estimated 10 per cent of people with SAD have ever been hospitalized.

Today, in the coffee bars of Finland, land of the midnight sun, you can order a coffee and a 'shot' of light – a special bright light at the table to lift your mood. London's Young Vic Theatre introduced its own light café, with large bright light panels at the tables. In Sweden, every building must have nuclear fall-out shelters, so all new buildings, including churches, have cellars with several feet of concrete and heavy lead-lined doors. However, as the cold war has receded, and therefore the nuclear threat, these Scandinavian cellars have had full-spectrum lights installed. You will commonly find Swedish citizens basking in their cellars under their full-spectrum lights. Switzerland funds research into light therapy.

Germany restricts the use of cool white limited-spectrum fluorescent bulbs in public buildings because of their distorted spectral output. Russia uses light therapy to boost productivity and reduce absenteeism in the workplace. Coalminers, for example, have to spend half an hour a day unclothed in natural light or under full-spectrum artificial lighting, which has been shown to prevent and treat black lung disease. Russian researchers have also documented that the body's tolerance to environmental pollutants and the effectiveness of immunization are increased by exposure to full-spectrum light.

Research by Dr George Brainard at the University of Pennsylvania has shown that people without SAD can dramatically improve their handling of stress under extended work conditions of 30-hour shifts when exposed to bright, white, fluorescent light. In both Russia and Germany, at work sites where individuals are engaged in shiftwork activity, the law mandates that full-spectrum lighting be used. Some American companies have noticed that workers are more productive, accurate and less likely to take absence in environments that use this type of lighting.

The benefits of light are not limited to humans. In a zoo in New York state, fertility soared after sunlight-simulating lights were installed in an effort to stop vandalism. Cougars, geese, sheep, deer, bear, wallaby and the chimpanzee all became pregnant.

Bright light therapy (BLT)

BLT is the most established treatment for SAD and consists of looking at special broad-spectrum bright lights from 30 minutes to 3 hours a day, generally in the early morning hours. It is believed to work by reducing or stopping the production of melatonin, while stimulating the brain to make more serotonin.

Light devices are becoming more powerful and portable and less expensive, resulting in increasingly wider use. This is usually done by means of a lightbox, though dawn simulators are also becoming popular and seem to be effective (see below).

The light needs to be especially bright – much brighter than an ordinary room light, which may only be around 200 to 700 lux. The intensity of light necessary for the treatment of SAD is from 2,500 or 3,500 to 10,000 lux.

Sally's doctor referred her to a psychiatrist who recommended daily exposure to bright light.

It really worked. As the lightbox manufacturers said, within two to three days I started noticing changes. I felt lighter and more energetic, and my food cravings diminished. I had so much more energy – on the third morning I looked out of the window, and suddenly thought, 'It's quite a nice day, why haven't I been for a walk for so long?' I found myself doing jobs I'd been putting off, had a lot more interest in making the house nice – I revamped the sitting room, got new curtains and big cushions for the sofa and generally made the place cosy for the winter. Whereas before I had wanted to stay in bed and just run down to the kitchen for endless snacks, now life expanded.
Sally

Jon found the first change he noticed was that colours began to seem brighter.

I use lightboxes regularly in the autumn and winter. Without lightboxes or some other kind of treatment, my life would not happen during the winter. I'm doing a very intensive course in the evenings as well as a day job and I simply cannot afford to let the time go by while I curl up in a corner, just wanting to sleep and eat, which was what happened before. At the moment I can't afford to let one day go – every moment is vital if I'm to get the qualification I'm aiming for.

When I started, the actual depression took about ten days to lift, but I felt changes in myself well before that – in fact, physically, I felt different every day and I wasn't quite sure what was going on. Now, at the end of the day in winter, I am tired, but it's a healthy tiredness that comes from doing things all day – not that unnatural tiredness I had before that made everything an effort.
Jon

For Jon, light treatment alone was enough. Sally did not rely on light treatment, but took other action to combat her SAD. At work, she rearranged her office so that her seat was closer to the window. She took daily walks to get the benefit of whatever sunlight there was. Although she still looked forward to the spring, she felt relieved that winter had lost its terrible hold.

Light therapy devices

Light sources are available commercially, though they are not available on the NHS (see the Useful addresses section at the back of the book).

The lightbox

The most common devices used for bright light therapy are fluorescent lightboxes that produce a light intensity of 2,500 to 10,000 lux while you sit around 30 to 90 cm (up to 3ft) away. Full-spectrum light is not necessary, as the intensity is the most important factor, but a balanced-spectrum light, minus UV-B emissions, is considered ideal.

Most lightboxes can easily be kept on a table or any other place where you normally spend some part of your day, such as a desk by a computer workstation, a dining room table or an exercise room.

Jon gave his father-in-law a lightbox for Christmas. As he is a writer, he kept it on routinely while working and, though he didn't have SAD, said he enjoyed the effect.

As with all light treatment, it is important not to stare directly into the lights because then there is the possibility of eye damage. Some people may be instructed to look at the lightbox briefly at regular intervals, though, for many, this doesn't seem to be necessary. The light does penetrate the eyes obliquely and even passes through closed eye-lids. Small lightboxes are available for taking to work or when travelling.

Some manufacturers will allow a trial period of two weeks or so, which should be enough to see if you benefit or not.

Light visors

These are worn on the head, much like a baseball cap, and have the obvious advantage of being much more convenient, delivering light from above the eyes and allowing you to carry on with normal activities. They produce white light with no UV and allow for mobility.

The disadvantage of these devices is that they are battery powered, which means the batteries need to be replaced from time to time and they seem to be less powerful and successful than lightboxes. However, some people find that using a visor for just 20 to 40 minutes a morning is enough. Others use a combination of visors and boxes to suit their routine.

When to use it

Light therapy is most helpful used daily in winter, starting in early autumn or even in August for some SAD sufferers. Some work has shown that starting treatment early in the year may help eliminate symptoms altogether, giving you a SAD-free winter. Conversely, the later light therapy is started, the more time may be needed to see results. Light therapy often starts working within one to three days. If you do not feel any better after two weeks, consult your doctor or other healthcare provider for further help.

Most people stop using light therapy in the spring as brighter natural light returns. However, you may find you continue to benefit from using the lightbox in spring and summer if there has been a run of rainy or cloudy weather.

Studies show that light therapy is most effective when used in the morning. Most people find that a session between 6 and 8 a.m., with perhaps another session in the afternoon between 3 and 7 p.m., works although this extra session can cause insomnia. Some find light therapy before bed helpful, but, again, this is likely to cause insomnia in most people.

The more powerful the lightbox, the shorter the session that will be needed. Generally, 20 to 30 minutes with a lightbox producing 10,000 lux (or one hour a day at 5,000 lux) is the average 'dose' that produces positive improvements.

As a rough guideline, whether you are a morning or an evening person may affect when it is best for you to use light treatment.

- For night owls (or those with DSPS – delayed sleep phase syndrome – to use its medical name). If you have trouble waking up in the morning and often feel sluggish for hours after awakening, even if you have slept longer than usual, you may benefit from an early morning session between 6 and 8 a.m.
- For morning people ('larks' or those with ASPS – advanced sleep phase syndrome). If you are at your most alert in the morning, possibly becoming tired around lunchtime, and often going to bed early from choice, you may benefit from a 30-minute session at 10,000 lux between 3 and 7 p.m. Short, periodic sessions throughout the afternoon at high intensity or longer exposure at lower intensity may also be considered. You may not benefit from a second session in the morning.

It may take some experimenting to find exactly what time of day suits you best, but, generally, it is recommended that you take your light medicine at the same time every day.

Once you start feeling better, you may be able to cut down on treatment time or even miss it out some days. Most people seem to be able to miss a couple of days without ill effects, but, by the third day without light therapy, symptoms may return.

Dawn/dusk simulators

A dawn simulator is like an alarm clock that works by faking a dawn. The device emits gradually brightening light half an hour before you wake up. This suppresses the production of melatonin in a natural way.

Visual stimulation is a more soothing way to wake up than the traditional shrill alarm clock. Also, unlike audio stimulation, the dawn helps set our biological clock to wake at the same time every day.

Research was conducted at the New York State Psychiatric Institute to find the effect dawn and dusk conditions has on SAD. A computer was used to simulate the gradual appearance of dawn and the gradual disappearance of light in the evening in a pattern characteristic of spring. During the winter months, the light disappears or appears pretty abruptly. It was found that, when subjected to this gradual simulated dawn, SAD sufferers reported substantial improvement, as good as following the full photo-therapy. Blood tests revealed that the dawn simulation resulted in cutting off the production of melatonin and restored the circadian rhythm. When exposed to the artificial dusk simulation, the patients experienced good, deep sleep. It almost appeared like 'a pleasant hypnotic sensation'.

The simulation of dawn and dusk has great potential in the treatment of SAD and more work is proceeding along these lines. The simulators are based on the premise that our ancestors awoke according to the rhythms of natural light (though farm workers did get up in the dark to do some chores by lamplight).

Dawn/dusk simulators appear to be most effective for those with mild symptoms, those who did not succeed with bright light therapy and those who have had success with bright light therapy but still have difficulty waking up. However, some people have found them to be as effective as light treatment, if not more so, and feel the benefits immediately.

The simulators may be particularly good for teenagers who dislike hanging around in front of a lightbox and have difficulty waking up. One study showed that 12 out of 12 teenagers found it easier to wake up with a dawn simulator (and their parents agreed).

These devices may also help to improve the quality of sleep. Another study showed that people who used them fell asleep sooner the following night.

Rachel, a 27-year-old lawyer, had suffered depression, which she called a 'predictable darkness', all and every winter since she was 17. She also got hungrier than usual and tended to crave sweets in the evening. In spite of sleeping for 10 or 11 hours, she still felt tired during the day and lost interest in her usual activities. She often felt irritable, worthless and guilty, didn't want to see her friends and her sex drive was very low.

After three weeks of using a dawn simulator, she felt much better. Her mood was 'almost as good as in the summer' and she had far more energy. Her appetite returned to normal, she slept less and was much more productive at work.

Paul, a 53-year-old who complained of depression from November to April, recalled having had winter depression for almost 20 years. In addition to feeling down, Paul lost pleasure in doing most everyday things. He craved food much more, ate more and usually put on about 20 pounds each winter. Paul often woke during the night and was unable to fall back to sleep for several hours. He would get out of bed and spend hours reading or surfing the Net. He was often tired during the day and had trouble concentrating on things, such as work and reading the newspaper. He tended to be more tense and irritable during the winter and more likely to worry about his physical health.

Paul was given dawn simulation therapy at home before waking up. After three weeks, his mood improved, he regained interest in his work and other activities and was able to sleep through the night. His appetite was still a little greater than in the summer, but, overall, he felt much better.

Which therapy?

Researcher David Avery found that lightbox therapy led to an 80 per cent reduction in symptoms, a dawn simulator 70 per cent, Prozac 55 per cent and evening light therapy 33 per cent.

Generally, lightboxes are regarded as more powerful and effective than visors, though the latter are more convenient. Dawn simulators are the most convenient form of light therapy of all as they work while you sleep.

Jon used the visor in the morning when he woke up and wore it for 20 minutes while lying in bed chatting with his wife. Then he used a 10,000 lux lightbox, which he considered more powerful, in the afternoon at 4.30 p.m. for 30 minutes. As he was doing a course, there was always reading to catch up on so he would do this then or he would just 'stare into the box and use the time to chill out and just relax'. Jon added that people without seasonal depression dislike the light and find it irritating. His wife found it gave her a headache, whereas he 'soaked it up'.

Marta came to the UK from Brazil and found herself falling into the familiar pattern of SAD sufferers: in September and October she would begin to feel very down. She thought it was because she had come from a naturally sunny country to a darker, colder one, and supposed that SAD was something that only affected people from sunny countries. That was until she made friends with an English girl, Alison, who also suffered from SAD. Marta used a lightbox while Alison used a visor. The two swapped treatments for a while, but found little difference in their effectiveness.

When it doesn't work

Some people may find that they are not helped by bright light therapy and there are various reasons for this. It could be because you are not using the equipment properly – check with your doctor and the manufacturers of the lighting device. A support organization could also help (see the Useful addresses section at the back of the book).

It could also be that your depression has nothing to do with SAD, even though it may appear to or actually become worse in winter. For example, some people spend more time in the house in winter, suffering social isolation and concomitant depression as a result, or it could be a chronic depression for which other treatment is needed. Clinical depression may not respond to bright light therapy or at least not bright light alone. A study at the University of Alberta, Canada, showed that people recovering from severe depression recovered in 16.9 days if they were in a sunny ward, but took 19.5 days if they were in a dull ward – a difference of 2.6 days. However, these patients received other treatment for depression as well, including antidepressants and counselling.

If light therapy does not benefit you, it is important to consult your doctor. Sometimes light therapy works better when combined with other treatments.

Julie found that a lightbox helped, but only when she used it in combination with antidepressant medication (she took Cipramil) during winter. She said she could just about manage to get through with this, but did not feel that it was a proper substitute for sunlight and would only really feel herself when spring came again and she could halt her medication.

Carole suffered depression as well as SAD and took antidepressants all the year round, making use of a light visor as well during the darker months. She also attended a support group for people with depression and had some counselling.

Safety and side-effects

It is worth consulting your doctor before using light therapy to rule out the possibility that you have clinical depression. If you have the latter, it can easily be treated with modern medications, but won't respond to light.

Also check with your doctor before starting light therapy if you have:

- an eye disorder, such as glaucoma, cataracts or detached retina;
- any sort of depression that lasts the entire year, even if it gets worse in winter;
- a rash, high temperature or any other symptoms of illness, in which case you might have an infection;
- another condition that necessitates taking medication – some drugs can make you photosensitive, as can contact lenses, in which case you may need to start on a lower 'dose' of light treatment.

Research seems to indicate that UV rays are not essential in light treatment – indeed, they are generally screened out of light therapy equipment or reduced to low, safe levels.

Generally, light therapy is considered a safe form of treatment, with mild, temporary side-effects experienced only by a minority. Irritability, agitation or excitability, slight nausea, mild headache and eyestrain for the first few days appear to be the main side-effects. These can be reduced by sitting further away from the light or by reducing the length of the session time or both. Consistent, long-term overuse may arouse mania or feelings of being 'high' in a tiny proportion (around 1 per cent) of users.

If you are on antidepressants, it may be possible to reduce the dose once light therapy has been established and is effective. Again, consult your doctor about the best way to do this as reducing or giving up medication without medical supervision can be dangerous.

Can light treatment help other conditions?

Those with dyslexia can be helped to read comfortably by wearing tinted glasses or overlays as black and white is often too harsh for them to see clearly. Specialist optometrists use the Intuitive Colorimeter (invented by Dr Arnold Wilkins) to evaluate individual colours of the tinted glasses that improve reading and help to prevent migraines.

Another recent use of light therapy, developed for the military, involves shining light on to a non-visual part of the retina to prevent sleepiness over a period of 48 hours. Curiously, the use of strobed light in a sleeper's eyes has been found to stop snoring. These last and other non-therapeutic uses of light, howerver, are hardly to be applauded as they will lead to imbalances in the body.

There are very many impressive medical uses of light, but we shall focus here on its application in complementary medicine:

- ultraviolet light is used to treat psoriasis;
- full spectrum or blue light cures jaundice in newborns by chemically breaking down excess bilirubin in the skin;
- a study of two women with post-natal depression showed that light therapy did help;
- another study showed that abstinent alcoholics treated with light therapy in the form of a dawn simulator found it easier to stay sober, so raising the possibility that light therapy might be used to help treat those who abuse drugs and alcohol;
- some research suggests that keeping a light on all night mid-cycle may help women with long menstrual cycles (those lasting more than 34 days).

Although the claims for light therapy are very far-ranging, this whole area needs more research as many of these studies are small one-off affairs.

Other types of light therapy

At the moment, light therapy for SAD is via the eyes because, as we saw earlier, this is how the pineal gland is activated. However, one study showed that it is possible to alter a person's circadian rhythm by shining light on the back of the knees, suggesting that treatment via the skin might be a possibility for the future.

Coloured light therapy – introduced in America in the nineteenth century – still remains experimental and has undergone far less research than bright light therapy. However, more and more specific frequencies are proving to be effective for a growing number of conditions – whether or not SAD is one of them remains to be seen.

Other types of light therapy include brief strobic photostimulation (BSP), which is exposure to rhythmic coloured light, and this is often used together with other forms of therapy such as counselling. There are also red light therapy and flickering light/polarized light therapy.

Coloured strobe light therapy is used to assist psychotherapy and enhance vision and learning ability. This type of light therapy should only be conducted by a qualified therapist or doctor. Such therapies are not usually recommended for people with SAD, however. Bright light treatment, which counters the light deprivation, remains the most effective and best-researched treatment to date.

Coloured light therapy often blends into colour therapy. In colour therapy, certain colours are believed to have certain properties that affect the individual in certain ways. For example, red is believed to stimulate the nervous system which raises our readiness for action. Blue is supposed to help lower blood pressure and induce calm. Certain colours are used routinely in public life, such as Baker-Miller pink – a shade of pink used in prisons and other institutions to reduce aggression and violence. However, this is another area where much more research is needed to assess the impact of colour on people with SAD.

Other light therapies also blend into complementary therapies. Laserpuncture is a development of acupuncture, which traditionally

77

uses needles to stimulate acupuncture points all round the body. Developed in Russia, instead of needles low-energy laser beams are used to stimulate acupuncture points. This may help with conditions such as stress that worsen SAD, but the therapy has not been definitively tested as a treatment for SAD itself.

8
Nutrition

Can the right food help to rebalance your brain chemicals and boost your mood? Yes, according to some specialists in nutrition. Their suggestions fall in with the latest thinking on healthy eating and form a diet plan that can be followed all the year round for optimum health.

As already mentioned, people with SAD tend to crave and eat more simple carbohydrates – both sweets and starches – and may put on weight in winter. This annual weight gain needs to be monitored as obviously staying within reasonable weight limits is better for your overall long-term health. Emotional or comfort eating is also common – eating in response to difficult situations, anxiety, depression and loneliness. So, for people with SAD, it is important to plan what to eat and when.

The urge to binge on simple carbohydrates is thought to be a form of self-medication, in that it can be a way of increasing brain chemicals, such as serotonin. The problem with simple carbohydrates, such as white bread, buns and sweets, is that their effect is temporary and only leads to further cravings for the same kinds of foods.

By balancing protein and complex carbohydrates, many nutritionists believe it is possible to raise levels of serotonin by means of your diet and build a more resilient brain chemistry that will help resist cravings and the urge to overeat. This chapter looks at the best way to monitor diet so as to control mood and cravings.

Winter weight gain and how to tackle it

It is worth looking this one squarely in the face because, though dispiriting, it is possible to do something about it.

In evolutionary terms, storing fat in our bodies for winter made sense as it could have made the difference between survival and death. Many centuries ago, when food was scarce in cold weather, the shortening days were a signal to the body to slow down its metabolism and start storing fat for the winter.

Less light and lowered levels of serotonin also set up a craving for carbohydrates, which increased insulin levels. Higher levels of insulin helped move calories into fat cells (store fat), and also lower blood sugar, so increasing hunger. This combination was an effective survival technique in the cold. The extra carbohydrates would have been mopped up by our bodies striving to keep warm (there was no central heating then) and by the physical labour we had to do for life to go on.

Nowadays, however, instead of food being scarce, winter sees the arrival of the biggest eating institution of the year, Christmas. Instead of living off our stored body fat as we chop wood, hunt and beat our washing clean in the stream, it is all too easy to spend the time adding to it while driving to work or sitting in front of the TV. As well as the food being there, the cold and dark militate against going out for exercise. The result: weight gain.

The problem with winter weight gain is that it is not always lost during the summer – or else not completely. Over the years, this has a cumulative effect, so that, for example if you gain 4.5 kg (10 lbs) each winter and lose 3.6 kg (8 lbs) each summer, you are still gaining 0.9 kg (2 lbs) each year. That's an extra stone every six years and a health threat that deserves to be considered carefully.

The good news is that winter weight gain can be tackled as part of a year-long eating plan that aims to address cravings. The key to this, according to the latest research, is a combination of protein and complex carbohydrates.

The protein and carbohydrate combination – why your brain needs it

By understanding more about how food affects the brain, it is possible to gain more control over eating. Essentially, different types of food work on different brain chemicals.

Protein

Protein feeds your body the amino acid tryptophan, which is then used by the brain to make serotonin. Foods rich in tryptophan include any protein, such as chicken, turkey, milk and dairy products, fish, eggs, beans and pulses. If you are watching your weight, choose poultry, lean meat and low-fat cheeses, such as cottage cheese, feta and Edam. Goat's cheese, Cheddar and Parmesan all have a high fat content.

Protein has a number of other functions that help stabilize body chemistry. It boosts production of dopamine – another of the brain chemicals thought to be lacking in people with SAD. Dopamine helps us initiate movement and express emotions. Protein also helps stabilize blood sugar levels.

Carbohydrates

Boosting serotonin levels is not a matter of simply going on a high-protein diet. Your body also needs carbohydrates, because they help tryptophan to pass into the brain via the bloodstream. A key point here is that they should be 'complex' or 'unrefined' carbohydrates, such as potatoes, wholemeal bread, oats and brown rice and pasta. If you are being careful about your weight, eating lots of vegetables will give you the carbohydrates you need without adding too many calories. Try to avoid simple carbohydrates, such as cakes, biscuits and sweets. The reason for this is that they do not have a long-term effect on serotonin because they can boost insulin too much, causing rebound low blood sugar and, in turn, lowered levels of insulin.

A combination of carbohydrates and proteins is needed to help balance mood, though if you have SAD you may need more carbohydrates than most people in order to boost serotonin levels enough.

The sugar and alcohol factors

Research suggests that people with SAD appear to process sugar differently in winter than they do in summer or after light therapy in winter. Given the craving for sweets so many people with SAD have and the links between alcoholism and SAD (see Chapter 4) – and the lack of serotonin is implicated in both conditions – it is interesting to consider the work of Kathleen DesMaisons here. A specialist in sugar and alcohol addiction, Dr DesMaisons has worked out an eating plan designed to combat cravings for sugar and alcohol that boosts levels of the brain chemicals serotonin, dopamine and beta-endorphin naturally.

It is Dr DesMaisons' belief that people who crave sugar or alcohol probably have an inherent extra need for serotonin. They may also lack other brain chemicals, including dopamine and beta-endorphin. For example, both sugar and alcohol cause a release of the neurotransmitter beta-endorphin, which produces a sense of well-being. People with certain brain chemistries, according to Dr DesMaisons, respond to the effect of sugar in a bigger way than other people. She explains the mechanisms which lead to imbalances of brain chemicals, such as 'priming', whereby eating or drinking a small amount of a substance (like sugar) can make a person want more. In summary, the more sugar is eaten, the more beta-endorphin is released, causing the brain to compensate for this 'excess' by shutting down some of its beta-endorphin receptors. The result is low beta-endorphin levels which may cause feelings of depression, tearfulness and low self-esteem, as well as further craving for sweets.

To combat low levels of serotonin and other brain chemicals, Dr DesMaisons suggests that you:

- keep a food diary;
- have a breakfast with protein;
- have three meals a day;
- eat protein with every meal;
- eat complex carbohydrates;
- reduce or eliminate sugar and simple carbohydrates – also consider considering cutting down or eliminating alcohol, too, because as well as being full of sugar, it is also a natural depressant;
- eat a baked potato (with its skin) as a pre-bedtime snack to boost insulin production that, in turn, helps raise serotonin levels while you sleep, but eat it without protein – say, with margarine or olive oil – as protein interferes with the serotonin-building process. The potato can be a small one.

This chapter looks at some of these suggestions (as well as suggestions from other nutritionists), but, for more details, read *Potatoes Not Prozac*, listed in the Further reading section at the back of this book.

Eat breakfast

It is well documented that people eating 2,000 calories-worth of food in the morning lose 0.9 kg (2 lbs) per week, while those eating the same amount of calories after 6 p.m. gain weight. Breakfast kickstarts your metabolism, which tends to slow down anyway in winter. By not having breakfast, you give your brain the message that you are in starvation mode. The result is that your metabolism slows down even more and conserves its fat stores as much as possible.

Try a protein and complex carbohydrate combination at breakfast, with some fresh fruit or juice. If you've eaten nothing but toast and coffee for years, it may be a bit of an effort, but your physiology could well appreciate the results. The chances are that you will feel fuller, more energetic and less likely to crave sugary snacks at 11 a.m. Here are some suggestions:

- hash browns and a poached egg or omelette,
- porridge with a handful of raspberries or blackberries (these are low in sugar, but choose your favourite fruit if you prefer);
- raw oats, sunflower seeds, half a chopped banana, skimmed milk or plain yogurt;
- lean bacon and wholemeal bread for a bacon butty with slices of tomato;
- baked beans on toast (choose a low-sugar variety);
- cottage cheese with chopped fruit;
- two slices of wholemeal or multigrain toast with peanut butter or yeast extract;
- two boiled eggs, a slice of wholemeal toast and a citrus fruit salad, such as grapefruit, orange and so on;
- wholemeal pitta bread stuffed with Edam cheese and lettuce;
- wholemeal flour pancake with chopped fresh fruit and yogurt.

The importance of food planning

For people with SAD, planning what and when to eat can be especially helpful. This includes thinking ahead to times when you know you will be vulnerable. For example, if a work lunch means eating fatty or sugary food, you may be better off taking raw vegetables and a cottage cheese salad to nibble.

Plan your shopping, too, so that you head straight for the healthy foods and ignore the aisles which stock sweets and cakes. The old advice not to shop when you're hungry may not apply here. If you go to the shops and you're hungry, focus on how good and fresh those vegetables and other healthy foods will taste once you get them back home. Bear in mind the habit factor, too – it is supposed to take 30 days to change a habit!

Coping with cravings

Once you are eating three meals a day with a good balance of protein and complex carbohydrates, you may find that cravings diminish of their own accord. Here are a few more tips to help you battle against the urge to overeat and win.

- Increase your protein intake. Although you may be eating protein at every meal, it may not be enough for your needs. Sometimes extra protein can help fend off cravings for less healthy foods.
- Eat a small amount of what you want when you want it. One to three pieces of chocolate when you crave it may be all that is needed. Fighting against the craving can lead to overeating later on. Nutritionist Debra Waterhouse (see the Further reading section at the back of the book) says that eating small amounts of the food we crave can help balance brain chemicals and boost serotonin levels. Other nutritionists do not agree, saying that a little now may lead to a lot later. Another idea is the traditional one of keeping sugar and simple carbohydrates as part of regular meals, eating them as dessert after or with protein. It's a question of finding out what suits you. If a little chocolate leads to a binge, it may be better to avoid it altogether.
- Rest – you may be confusing hunger with tiredness.
- Distract yourself. Try to keep busy if you feel a craving coming on. Call a friend, read a book or do some task around the house that needs doing.
- Try to wait for 20 minutes before giving in. Then wait another ten minutes.
- A technique from Ayurvedic medicine is to drink a mug of hot water with a little lemon or lime juice and a teaspoon of honey stirred into it to see if it is emotional or real hunger. If you are not really hungry, this can give you a taste of sweetness and may help fill you up.

- Schedule in your cravings. For example, if you know you tend to binge in the evening, set out one portion of the food you're going to allow yourself – a slice of chocolate cake, say – and allow yourself to enjoy that. Back it up with healthy nibbles, such as grapes, carrot sticks and so on.
- Identify your danger times. Common low points are mid-afternoon around 4 p.m. and evenings. Then, change your routine accordingly. Arrange to meet a friend or go out.
- Try to identify any emotional sources of eating and deal with them. Look at situations and stresses that make it more likely that you'll eat or may trigger you into comfort eating, such as when you're busy at work or alone.

To snack or not to snack

Given the urge to nibble that many people with SAD have, how good are snacks? There is a case for and against here.

If one nibble leads to another and then another and snacking does not seem to satisfy the uncontrollable hunger that some people with SAD report, it may be better to try and stick to just three meals a day, plus a snack of complex carbohydrates at bedtime. Schooling your body to wait for meals may, after a few days, help lessen that feeling of round-the-clock hunger.

On the other hand, some nutritionists believe that snacks are important and you should eat every three to four hours to keep brain chemicals and blood sugar boosted and avoid tiredness, irritability and later overeating. If you tend to suffer from premenstrual tension, having a carbohydrate snack no more than three hours apart may be especially important to help maintain blood sugar levels.

It's a question of finding out what suits you. The type of food you snack on is just as important as what you eat at mealtimes. Try to avoid sugar, which may indeed lead to more eating than you had planned. Bear in mind that snacks do not have to be huge – sometimes, a couple of crackers may be enough. Try having just half what you feel you want to eat. Snacks could include:

- the breakfast suggestions given above;
- egg and cress sandwich;
- rye crackers with low-fat cheese;
- tortilla or bread wrap, chopped tomato, hot sauce and Edam cheese;

- fruit;
- seeds;
- handful of almonds and two dried figs;
- apple and cheese sticks;
- baked potato with tuna fish and cottage cheese or beans and a grating of Edam or tomato chopped with onion and a touch of chilli;
- wholemeal bagel with low-fat cream cheese and salmon;
- wholemeal pitta bread with tinned black beans, olives, feta cheese and salad;
- instant soups or meals (those you just add boiling water to), such as pea or lentil soup.

Cut down your calorie intake a little

Starving yourself is not only painful but also ineffective. As with missing breakfast, it sends a message to your body that it is vital to hang on to its fat stores. Your metabolism then slows down and you keep the fat instead of losing it.

However, cutting down your calorie intake just a little over time will work. It is surprising how easy it can be to shave calories off your daily intake so that you hardly realize it is happening. For example, not eating a digestive biscuit saves you 70 calories a time, while avoiding a glass of wine saves you 100 calories. Not putting margarine on your bread saves you around 70 calories a slice. Even if you only do this once a day, what you don't eat can amount to quite a bit of weight in the course of a year.

Other dietary ways to feel better

- Cut down on or avoid coffee – several studies have linked depression with a high intake of caffeine, showing that depressed patients tend to consume fairly large amounts of caffeine and that the higher the intake, the more severe the depression tends to be. If you drink four or more cups a day, try substituting decaffeinated coffee or mineral water.
- Avoid processed foods that contain artificial colouring and preservatives.

- Pay attention to see if any foods cause allergic reactions, tiredness, heaviness, digestive upsets or any other adverse reactions (keeping a food diary will help).
- Eat oily fish, such as tuna, salmon and herring, once or twice a week. Oily fish is rich in the omega-3 type of polyunsaturated fat and it is good to boost your consumption of this fat as low levels may increase your vulnerability to depression.
- A balanced, varied diet with plenty of fresh fruit and vegetables will ensure that you get many of the vitamins and minerals you need. However, taking a multivitamin and mineral supplement will provide a good nutritional basis and prevent any imbalances from depleting your body of any one vital substance. Individual supplement needs are best discussed with a qualified health practitioner, such as a nutritionist, but supplementation specifically for SAD is discussed in Chapter 10.

9
Exercise and SAD

After light therapy, exercise is the most frequently recommended treatment for SAD, especially if it is done in daylight. Exercise treats both body and mind and is well known for its success. One study found that exercising for two hours a morning from 6 a.m. led to significant improvement in depression for people with SAD. Luckily, this level of exercise may not be necessary in order to benefit. You don't have to spend hours in the gym or start running marathons. Recent thinking on exercise is that brisk walking and getting more physical activity into your daily life can be good for you. This is good news, given that the last thing most SAD sufferers feel like doing is vigorous physical activity.

> Normally, I love exercise – I work out regularly at the gym, do weight training and swim three times a week with my wife – but, when I was in the grip of SAD, I just couldn't do it. I was too tired, exhausted all the time. Until I had light therapy, I just couldn't get started on any exercise.
> *Jon*

> Walking kept me going while I was in the depths of depression. No matter how bad I felt, I always felt a tiny bit better if I got outside and went for a walk in the fresh air. Once the antidepressants kicked in, my energy came back and I wanted to be with people, so I joined an evening yoga group. That would have been unthinkable with SAD.
> *Marta*

Marta and Jon's words highlight the fact that, for people with SAD, exercise may be more effective if it is combined with some other kind of treatment. Many combine exercise with other forms of help, such as medication, light therapy and changes to their diet. However, given the power of exercise to affect mood, any amount you can manage is worth trying. People who lead inactive lives are twice as likely to suffer depression.

The majority of the physiological benefits of exercise can occur in as little as a few days. These are immense. As well as banishing depression, regular exercise has been linked with a lower risk of breast cancer, reduction in the risk of stroke and a boost to your immune system. Exercise stimulates the thyroid gland, improving its functioning and thus making your metabolism work more effectively. Regular exercise reduces appetite and so makes you less likely to binge on carbohydrates.

Long-term regular exercise programmes, along with the right diet, are also enormously helpful in preventing obesity and type 2 diabetes – reducing the incidence of the latter by at least a third. This last point is important because, if you become and remain overweight as a result of SAD, you are unfortunately at increased risk of diabetes, as well as other health conditions. Exercise can also help lower your blood pressure, cut down or stop smoking, raise your HDL (good) cholesterol, promote bone health and reduce the risk of some cancers. Last but not least for people with SAD, it helps you sleep better.

Alison found that once she got started on light therapy and took up swimming again, her sleeping improved enormously.

I would fall asleep very naturally and sleep deeply and well, but without that feeling of heaviness I used to have. Waking up was a pleasure. I'd lie in bed and listen to the wind or the rain or whatever and it would be quite nice and cosy, nice to come round and good to be alive – not that awful feeling of, 'Oh no, another day, how am I going to get up?'
Alison

Exercise in the light

A number of studies have shown that, for people with SAD, exercising in the light is the key factor in improving mood.

In a preliminary study of women with SAD, exercising while exposed to light was more likely to be associated with fewer seasonal depressive symptoms than was exercising involving little light exposure.

In a controlled study, 120 people who worked indoors were tested to see what was most effective at improving depression and other aspects of health. They did fitness training two or three times a week while exposed to either bright light (2,500–4,000 lux) or ordinary light (400–600 lux). Compared to relaxation training, which was used as a placebo (something that was not meant to have any effect), exercise in bright light improved general mental health, social functioning, symptoms of depression and vitality, while exercise in ordinary light improved only vitality.

Even if there is no sun, you will still benefit from the daylight, which can help boost levels of serotonin and so make you feel better. Obviously opportunities for this are cut down in winter, but there are ways to manage it. Short bursts work best for some – a brisk ten-minute walk in the morning, at lunchtime and in the afternoon or a longer 20 to 30-minute session at lunchtime. If you can't manage to get out, try to exercise near a window, a bright lamp or your lightbox, if you have one.

Starting out

It is important to realize that you can start feeling better after one bout of exercise. Researchers at Indiana University in the US found a significant lessening of depression that lasted for at least two hours after moderate exercise. This shows that any kind of exercise is better than nothing. If you do feel very lethargic, try to increase your daily activity levels by a small amount – even by just five minutes a day to start with.

Experts recommend taking at least 30 minutes of moderate to intense physical activity most days of the week, preferably daily. Research also shows that half an hour of aerobic exercise four times a week will help banish depression. Spread out over a day, this is not actually that much. Nor need it be strenuous or involve expensive equipment or special clothing. It can be done just by taking three, brisk ten-minute walks a day, which you can build into everyday activities, such as walking up the road to post a letter. Set small goals on a daily basis that are easily achievable.

Some other easy ways to get started could be:

- walking the children to school – it's good for them, too;
- washing the car, especially if you leave it further along the road so you have to walk to and fro with buckets of water;

- walking to the shops and back – carrying a couple of bags back helps, too, but they shouldn't be too heavy, to avoid straining your back;
- playing actively with your children – get a ball and spend ten minutes in the garden or park;
- gardening – plan for spring, dig the garden over in autumn and plant bulbs for spring or rake fallen leaves and, if bylaws allow, have a bonfire;
- parking further away from work and walking the rest of the way;
- cleaning the house, especially if you move from job to job as vigorously as possible – for example, do the hoovering, then clean the bathroom;
- using the house as a gym – run up and down the stairs when taking items up or down and tidy items away as you come across them rather than putting them all at the bottom of the stairs to be taken up later;
- reducing the amount of time you spend watching TV or at least vowing to do something physical during the commercials;
- creating an exercise mentality – do this in very small steps by leaving your exercise clothes and trainers on the bed or by the back door and putting them on when you get up (even if you end up not doing any exercise at all, it is still one small step towards it and helps to start create an exercise mentality);
- finding excuses to visit people – walking to see a friend can be a very effective antidepressant (see if you can find a book to lend or a jar of homemade jam from those late summer days when you had a bit more go and take them round to someone or just visit without an excuse);
- pushing back the barriers of 'being tired' – after doing your ten minutes or so of activity, see if you can push yourself to continue for another five minutes and so on, progressively, until both your body and mind become used to exercise.

How exercise helps lift mood

The effect of exercise, as we have seen, is to lift mood. It can achieve this as effectively as antidepressants in some cases and this fact is well documented.

Exercise stimulates the brain to release hormones called endorphins – the body's natural painkillers, which produce a sense of wellbeing. Endorphin production usually begins about 15 to 20 minutes into an exercise session and peaks after about 45 minutes.

Physical activity is also thought to have other important effects on the brain. As well as lifting mood, exercise boosts blood flow and oxygen supplies to the brain and so speeds up brain activity. This is important given the role of certain brain chemicals and the circadian rhythm – the biological clock (the suprachiasmatic nucleus, SCN for short) – in SAD.

In America, a Surgeon General's report contained the finding that, just as changes in brain chemistry can affect behaviour, so changes in behaviour can affect brain chemistry. Studies with animals suggest that permanent structural changes in the brain – including extra blood vessels and nerve endings – can result from regular exercise. It has also been found that brain wave activity is positively altered by exercise training and good physical fitness.

While more research is needed before the influence of exercise on the brain is fully understood, we know that disturbances of brain chemicals such as serotonin and dopamine have been implicated in depression and exercise may help normalize brain concentrations of these chemicals, so logic and experience point to exercise being good medicine for those with SAD.

What type of exercise?

As mentioned earlier, exercising in the light has been pinpointed as important for those with SAD. Research also suggests that aerobic physical activities – such as brisk walking and running – improve mental health for people with SAD. Repetitious movements – such as walking, running and cycling – increase levels of serotonin, so this type of exercise is important in the SAD scenario.

The best kind of exercise, though, is really the kind that you enjoy best as then you are most likely to keep it up. You also need to consider other factors, such as how sociable you are feeling and whether you would be more motivated and have most fun exercising with other people or prefer to go it alone. Exercise also needs to fit into your routine easily, especially on a dark winter's night when you don't feel like going out.

Aerobic activities, such as walking briskly or jogging, are those that speed up your heart rate and breathing. They help cardiovascular fitness. Activities for strength and flexibility help maintain your bones, such as carrying shopping, lifting weights, stretching, dancing or yoga.

Once you're exercising

Once you've got going, you may want to progress on to something moderately more demanding in terms of organization and a bit closer to a formal exercise session, but still not want to expend great amounts of energy. Here are some ideas.

- **Stretching** SAD and winter often involve a lot of huddling up to keep warm, so stretching out gives your body a chance to counteract this and remove any tension. If you don't fancy yoga, Pilates is very easy and safe. Consult your sports club, library or Yellow Pages for books, videos or classes.
- **Cycling** Instead of driving, use a bike for those short runs to the shops or to see people. It has the advantage of being outside as well.
- **Dancing** Dancing classes come in all shapes and sizes, from formal ballroom to Latin American, line dancing to flamenco and jazz exercise classes. Some areas have dance therapy classes or dance and drama sessions that can be used therapeutically or simply as a means of self-expression. Ask your local health centre for details. You could always simply put some music on, open the curtains and dance at home.
- **Exercising with friends** Get a group of friends together in the park and play frisbee or organize a trip to your nearest ice-skating rink. Exercising in a group for fun is far more effective than slogging it out alone. It may also make you stick to your plan rather than give yourself excuses for not doing it.
- **Swimming** As warmth seems to help SAD sufferers, ask around or experiment to find out which is the warmest pool near you, then try a few lengths.
- **Rebounding** Jumping up and down on a small trampoline in the privacy of your own home is easy to fit into most routines and

may be less daunting than an exercise bike. It is very helpful in kickstarting your metabolism. Inexpensive bouncers are easily available and can be used for five to ten minutes or more while watching the news, or some other programme you never miss.

- **Floating** If you don't feel like swimming, try floating. Research shows that time spent in a flotation tank benefits both hemispheres of the brain, making you more creative, imaginative and able to solve problems. It's also proven to be good for addictive behaviours, so it could help if you have been overeating. Ask at your local fitness centre or health shop or see the Useful addresses section at the back of the book.
- **Videos and cassettes** For those chilly days when you just can't bring yourself to go out, try one or more from the wide variety of these available. You could experiment with the ones at your local library or video shop to find one you enjoy. Ask a friend to join you.

Weight training

If you do want to exercise more seriously, weight training helps you burn more calories per minute of exercise than aerobic exercise, and the effect on your metabolism lasts longer. After weight training, the increased activity of your metabolism lasts minutes or even hours after you stop exercising. Over weeks or months, your general metabolic rate increases.

What about calories?

'Calories' can be a bit of a dirty word in slimming and fitness circles, as can 'weight'. Counting calories and trying to burn off a set number of calories or a certain amount of weight, is rather frowned on by many fitness and nutrition experts. It is thought of as being old fashioned, ineffective and putting too much pressure on people to set impossible goals and lose unrealistic amounts of weight. It is far better to think in terms of creating a long-term healthier lifestyle that incorporates exercise as a natural part of it.

This said, many people still think in terms of calories and many fitness and slimming centres offer calorie counters, allowing you to see how much exercise burns off how many calories (see below). If it is not taken too far, counting calories can be a helpful way to take the bull by the horns.

You need to burn off 3,500 calories more than you take in to lose 0.5 kg (1 lb). This sounds daunting, but, going back to the suggestion that you spend half an hour a day on brisk walking, perhaps broken down into three ten-minute slots, this alone is enough to burn 1,000 calories a week.

How many calories can you burn?

Here are some examples of the average numbers of calories burned by a person weighing 150 lbs ($10\frac{3}{4}$ stone or 68·25 kg) doing various types of moderate to intense activity:

Activities	Calories lost per hour
Bicycling at 6 mph (9.6 kph)	240
Bicycling at 12 mph (19.3 kph)	410
Jogging at 5 mph (8 kph)	740
Jogging at 7 mph (11 kph)	920
Running on the spot	650
Running at 10 mph (16 kph)	1,280
Swimming at 25 yards/min (22.8 m/min)	275
Swimming at 50 yards/min (45.7 m/min)	500
Tennis (singles)	400
Walking at 2 mph (3.2 kph)	240
Walking at 3 mph (4.8 kph)	320
Walking at 4 mph (6.4 kph)	440

Obviously, weight loss will be speeded up if you reduce the numbers of calories you take in at mealtimes and in between. It is far harder to lose calories by exercising than to consume them. Just think, walking for an hour uses up around the same number of calories as are provided by two slices of bread and butter! (Help with controlling cravings and eating a balanced diet is given in Chapter 8.)

10

Other treatments

While light therapy is the treatment of choice for SAD, a minority of
people find that thcy are not helped by it. Some people also find that
light therapy works better in combination with other treatments.
More research is needed to find which of these work best for SAD,
but some preliminary trials have pointed to a number of remedies as
being potentially helpful.

Drug therapy

How effective are antidepressants? Many of the people consulted for
this book said they had revolutionized their lives. Some used
medication for a short while, just to 'get them out of the hole', others
on a more long-term basis. Medication may be more effective when
used in combination with light therapy.

Jon tried antidepressants for three years before discovering light
therapy and gave up his medication because he felt well enough with
extra light alone. Marta took antidepressants in autumn and winter
alone. Carole took medication all year round as she suffered from
clinical depression as well as SAD. Sally took antidepressants for
five months one autumn, but felt so much better after realizing what
was going on and adjusting her lifestyle accordingly, that the
following year she no longer needed them.

However, there is some controversy as to whether the antidepressants really work or the improvements are due to the placebo effect
(all in the mind). This is because some research has shown that
active placebos (placebos that mimic the side-effects of the
antidepressants, such as a dry mouth and insomnia, that is pills with
no actual antidepressant drugs in them) work as effectively as real
antidepressants. It has also been found that reading self-help books
(like this one!) can be as effective as antidepressants – and work
faster.

This said, the modern SSRIs widely used for depression are
known to treat the seratogenic pathways of the brain and raise levels

of serotonin. The most commonly prescribed drugs for SAD are drugs that regulate the neurochemical serotonin – the selective serotonin re-uptake inhibitors (SSRIs). These include include the drugs fluoxetine (Prozac), paroxetine (Seroxat) and sertraline (Lustral). They may have fewer side-effects than older antidepressants, but they can still have side-effects, such as anxiety, stomach upsets, headache, insomnia and others. Tricyclic antidepressants and monoamine oxidase inhibitors have also been used successfully, but generally people experience more side-effects when taking these.

Psychotherapy

Psychotherapy is usually used concurrently with other forms of treatment. You and your therapist set goals based on your individual needs.

Forms of talk therapy that can be helpful include behavioural therapy, which may focus on unhelpful patterns (such as not paying bills when feeling depressed), and insight-orientated treatment. The latter is a long-term approach that focuses on resolving psychological conflicts and can be extremely helpful to those with SAD or, indeed, any form of depression. Family and couples therapy may be used at times because of the impact of SAD on people close to those afflicted with it.

Cognitive therapy – often recommended for people with SAD – seeks to help people change how they think about things. This therapy will focus especially on rigid negative beliefs or inner dialogues we may not be aware of. By using techniques to challenge a depressed person's assumptions, the therapist helps to change or modify their thinking. Such a view could be 'Everyone should like me.' The therapy would consist of learning to modify the belief to 'I enjoy people liking me but realize it's not always going to happen.'

The theory of cognitive therapy describes the role of faulty thinking in making us anxious and suggests a way to recover from it, via cognitive restructuring. According to Aaron Beck, who formulated key components of cognitive therapy, the ways in which we process information are governed by structures called schemata. These schemata are made up of rules for explaining incoming information and can have a powerful effect on how we experience and relate to the world. Treatment consists of correcting illogical schemata with new information that challenges these deep-set beliefs.

Biofeedback

Biofeedback, as the name suggests, is a technique that gives a person extra feedback about the state their body is in. It aims to 'tap into' connections in the brain between many different areas that are not usually taken advantage of and gain more control of automatic functions, such as heart rate, breathing, body fluid regulation and regulation of temperature and blood flow.

The feedback can take the form of an audible tone that varies in pitch, lights that turn on and off or a line on a computer screen. A common form of biofeedback, EMG biofeedback, provides the person with feedback on how tense their muscles are. If computerized biofeedback equipment is used, you will see a line or other image on a screen that represents your muscle tension. The therapist helps you relax your muscles and you can see the progress for yourself by watching the computer image change. You then try to do the same and then improve on it.

Vitamin D and calcium

As explained in Chapter 2, vitamin D is well known for its effects of helping to maintain normal calcium levels, but it also exerts an influence on the brain, spinal cord and hormone-producing tissues of the body that may be important to the regulation of mood.

One study found that mood improved in healthy people without SAD who received 400 or 800 IU per day of vitamin D for five days in late winter. However, vitamin D supplements have not been shown to help people with SAD, according to the small amount of research that has been done. A large study of women found that supplementation with 400 IU per day of vitamin D had no impact on the incidence of winter depression. Also, no difference in vitamin D levels has been observed between people with SAD and those without it. Further, the antidepressant activity of light therapy has been shown to be independent of changes in levels of vitamin D. So, the benefits of extra vitamin D on SAD remain unproven.

This is probably not an area to experiment with yourself, as vitamin D supplements are toxic if taken in excess. While 400–800

IU daily is a relatively safe dose, vitamin D is not easily eliminated from the body. The body's own synthesis of the vitamin, on the other hand, is self-regulating. It is much easier and safer (and cheaper) to simply get more daylight.

Vitamin D is available in some foods, the richest sources being cod liver oil and oily fish, such as sardines, herring, mackerel, tuna, salmon and pilchard, while eggs, liver and butter provide a little.

If you are concerned about your calcium levels, food sources of calcium include dairy products, such as milk, yogurt and cheese, canned fish, if you eat the bones, hard water, dried figs, green vegetables, sesame seeds, bread and flour.

Vitamin B12

Depression can be one of the first symptoms of vitamin B12 deficiency, so supplementation has been recommended for SAD. However, one clinical trial found that vitamin B12 (as cyanocobalamin) worked no better than a placebo in a double-blind trial (that is, neither group knew whether they were taking vitamin B12 or not). Another study, however, suggested that it might work better if taken three times a day rather than all at once.

It is always better to take any B vitamins as part of a vitamin B complex, to avoid imbalances, or as a natural supplement in the form of brewer's yeast. Food sources of B vitamins include oats, green leafy vegetables, pulses, whole grains and cereals, fortified breakfast cereals, fish and meat.

Serotonin and L-tryptophan

Serotonin itself cannot be taken in supplement form because it is actually produced in the brain but even if serotonin supplements were taken, it cannot be transported into the brain via the bloodstream. However, the substance the brain uses to make serotonin – the amino acid tryptophan – can be taken in supplement form.

A number of medical trials have shown that removing L-tryptophan from the diets of SAD patients who are feeling better in the summer or after light therapy brings about a relapse into a depressed state. These suggest that taking supplements might be helpful.

In other, small trials, 4 to 6 grams of L-tryptophan given in divided doses daily was as effective as light therapy. It has been suggested that L-tryptophan may be of particular use to people who do not benefit from light therapy. However, it has been shown to help those who are already receiving light therapy as well.

The acronym '5-HTP' stands for 5-hydroxytryptophan and this is a substance related to L-tryptophan that also increases serotonin production and has been used for its antidepressant effects. Although there is currently no research data on this, it may be useful in the treatment of SAD. Stick to the recommended dosage, however, if you do decide to try it as nausea can be a side-effect.

Melatonin

Because changes in melatonin levels are believed to be an important factor in SAD, there has been some experimentation to see if supplements of it could help.

Some work has suggested that small doses (0.25 mg) taken around 8 hours after waking may help to regularize sleeping and waking patterns and the circadian rhythm. On the whole, however, melatonin has been found to be ineffective and may even make things worse for people with SAD, reversing the benefits of light therapy and actually adding to a sluggish feeling so sufferers find hard to take.

St John's wort (Hypericum perforatum)

Taking St John's wort has resulted in around a 40 per cent improvement in symptoms according to research projects with people suffering from SAD, although some of this may be due to a placebo effect (believing it will make you feel better makes you feel better). It may be more effective if taken in conjunction with light therapy.

A herb well known for its antidepressant effect, St John's wort has a long history. The ancient Greeks believed that it had supernatural powers and its fragrance would cause evil spirits to fly away. The Romans must have been of the same view as they burned its leaves and flowers on Midsummer Day to rid them of evil spirits.

The plant was later dedicated to the world of Christianity when it was recognized that it bloomed close to John the Baptist's birthday (24 June). The black marks on the leaves were said to be a symbol of his beheading at the insistence of Herod's daughter, Salome.

St John's wort has undergone trials as a treatment for SAD. In one uncontrolled trial, people were given 900 mg per day as well as either bright light therapy (3,000 lux for two hours) or dim light therapy (300 lux for two hours) – a placebo. Both groups experienced significant improvement in their symptoms of depression and there was no difference between them. The authors concluded that St John's wort was beneficial with or without bright light therapy, but a placebo effect of the herb itself cannot be ruled out in this study.

Another uncontrolled study asked 300 SAD patients if they reported overall improvement in their depression while taking St John's wort. Some used light therapy as well as St John's wort, and they reported more improvement in how well they slept, but, overall their improvement was not significantly different from that of those using St John's wort alone.

More clinical trials are needed to clarify just how helpful St John's wort can be for SAD, but anecdotal evidence suggests that many people not only find it useful but rely on it to some extent. As before, how much of this is a placebo effect or psychological dependence and how much is a real improvement isn't clear.

You may need to allow around a week before your depression starts to lift. Be aware that you should avoid exposure to the sun while taking it as a side-effect of St John's wort is that it can cause photosensitivity in direct sunlight. Also, if you are taking any medication, you must check with your doctor before taking St John's wort as it interacts with some drugs. These mainly include indinavir, warfarin, cyclosporin, digoxin and theophylline. St John's wort may also interact with a wide range of other drugs, however, including oral contraceptives, anticonvulsants, SSRIs and triptan, used for migraine, so get advice.

Aromatherapy

In aromatherapy, many essential oils are used as antidepressants, including jasmine, rose, neroli, rosemary, melissa and lavender.

Aromatherapy combined with light therapy may help treat SAD, according to work by psychiatrist Teodor Postolache of Washington in the US. He suggests that there are links between the sense of smell and SAD. Dr Postolache found that the more depressed SAD people felt, the less accurate they were at identifying smells. However, in summer, they had a more acute sense of smell than people without SAD, suggesting a link between SAD and the sense of smell.

When you breathe in through your nose, the olfactory (smell) nerves are stimulated and there is a direct pathway from them to the brain's limbic system, which is involved with memory, emotion, mood, expression and instinctive behaviours, such as self-preservation.

In 'psycho-aromatherapy' – a word used by aromatherapists to describe the effects of oils on the psyche – it's crucial that the odour of the essential oil is welcomed. One study showed that a pleasant odour caused a wave of electrical activity in the right hemisphere of the brain, home of imagination, creativity and aesthetic awareness. Dr Postolache found that SAD patients seemed to be particularly bad at identifying smells by means of the right nostril (olfactory sensors in the right nostril send messages to the right side of the brain).

A sense of smell plays an important part in many animals' awareness of the seasons. Hamsters largely lose their sense of when to build nests and hibernate if they do not have olfactory bulbs. Given that, in the long distant past, resting during winter may have been important for survival, Dr Postolache suggests that, as humans evolved, we may have lost some genes, resulting in some loss of awareness of the seasons and our sense of smell. He speculates that people affected by seasonal changes also preserved this heightened sense of smell. In other words, SAD people are an evolutionary throwback whose survival mechanisms work too powerfully for the world in which we live today. This fits in with the idea of SAD as an exaggerated form of hibernation.

Ionizers

Ionizers are devices that work by releasing negative ions, which are molecules that each contain an extra electron, and these help clean the air. Some research has found that ionizers help reduce the irritation and depression of SAD, while improving energy levels.

One study on high-density negative ionization for people with SAD, showed a 50 per cent improvement or more for nearly 60 per cent of the people who received the high-density ionization. This contrasts markedly with the other group as only 15 per cent of those receiving low-density ionization had 50 per cent or greater improvement. There were no side-effects and all of the patients who responded to the therapy relapsed when ionization was discontinued.

Another study showed that high-density ionization was as effective as light therapy. Yet another study, however, showed that nearly twice as many (61 per cent) people using light therapy in the mornings completely recovered after four weeks than was the case for those who were just exposed to a deactivated negative ion generator and had no light therapy as 32 per cent of them made a complete recovery in the same time.

Marie, a 45-year-old who had suffered depression from late October until April for five years, was losing interest in most things, including socializing and sex. As with many SAD sufferers, her appetite grew and she craved stodgy food and sweets in the afternoon. Marie also suffered sleep disturbance, waking up in the middle of the night, and felt tired during the day, especially mid-afternoon – 'as if my arms and legs had weights on them'.

A friend suggested an ionizer and, after two weeks, Marie realized she was feeling much better. While she was not sure that her productivity at work was as high as in summer, she did feel that most of her interest in work, sex and socializing had returned to normal, along with her appetite, energy levels and ability to sleep soundly.

Other remedies

There are so many complementary and alternative therapies available that choosing one really is a matter of individual taste and experimentation. The following remedies have all been recommended for depression.

- Music is well known for its ability to affect physical conditions such as pain, muscle tone, blood pressure and heart rate. Music therapy may help people deal with some of the more negative feelings associated with SAD, such as anxiety, morbidity, uncertainty, low self-esteem and loneliness. It can take a wide range of forms, including song writing, singing, playing, listening, drumming, dance and musical puppet play.
- Laughter is said to release endorphins, which are brain chemicals that increase feelings of wellbeing and counteract SAD. Some hospitals have 'laughter therapy' programmes. The cheap multi-purpose 'drug' of laughing has been found to lower blood pressure, reduce stress hormones, increase muscle flexion and boost immune function. In countries such as India, laughing clubs – where members gather in the early morning for the sole purpose of laughing – are becoming popular. While no one can laugh to order, getting in some comic videos, having a laugh with a friend or just trying to see the funny side of life from time to time may all help.
- Listen to a tape of natural sounds or look at pictures of natural vistas in books or art galleries. According to the Johns Hopkins Medical Institution in the US, natural sounds, such as the gurgle of a brook, and sights, such as a mountain panorama, are highly effective at lifting mood and can even reduce discomfort during operations by 43 per cent.
- Have a sauna and remind your body what those hot summer days really feel like. Try to remember last summer in as much detail as possible while you're sitting there and visualize the return of those balmy days – it's only a matter of time. When you get home, write out your ten best memories of summer in a lovely notebook or on special paper, perhaps to share with your children.
- Light scented candles or burn oils with flowery scents or indulge in bunches of real flowers or a pot hyacinth.

- Visualization techniques can help lift you above your present mood. For example, visualize a ball of sunshine to help calm emotions, make you feel happier and relieve any stiff or painful areas, suggests consultant psychologist and hypnotherapist Phyllis Allen of the Derbyshire Royal Infirmary. Try visualization for more long-term purposes, too, such as setting life goals. Close your eyes and relax as much as possible and ask yourself how you would really like your life to be. Note any images that flash into your mind and write them down. Then, focus on them again in your head in as much detail as possible, to get a clear picture of what you want. At the end of each session, try to make at least one practical move towards achieving your goal. For example, if your dream is to own a house in the country, ring up some estate agents and have them send you some details or book a stay in the area of your choice.
- In Ayurvedic medicine, depression is seen as losing touch with the freedom of the deep inner self and relating too much to the outside world (an extreme form of 'object referral'). Treatment of depression is to try and rediscover your inner self, often by meditation or sitting in quiet thought, perhaps combined with gentle stretching exercises, such as yoga.

Breathing deeply

Shallow, constricted breathing can be a result of depression or make it worse by causing an inadequate supply of oxygen in the blood. Deep, regular breathing helps to increase the amount of oxygen that is reaching your lungs, blood, organs and cells, as well as relax your body and mind.

How to deepen your breathing

- Lie down with your back flat on the floor, with your knees bent and feet a small distance apart.
- Rest one hand on your stomach and the other hand on your chest.
- Inhale slowly and deeply through your nose, taking the breath into your stomach so that your hand feels it rise. Your chest should move slightly along with your abdomen. Exhale just as deeply and feel your abdomen and ribs move.

- Once you are comfortable with this, inhale deeply, then blow the air out gently through your mouth.
- Deep-breathe for five to ten minutes once or twice each day. This exercise can be done for up to 20 minutes at a time, whenever you feel the need to relax and focus your energy.

Conclusion

Seasonal affective disorder and viewing sunlight as health-giving can easily be classified as marginal, cranky or suspiciously anecdotal because it has not entered the medical 'canon' – that is, what we accept as true or regard as the hard facts of medicine. This is changing. SAD now has more than two decades of clinical research behind it and public interest is growing all the time. However, the 'winter blues', in many quarters, are still regarded wryly or with suspicion, despite clear evidence of the widespread distress they cause. The flavour of gloom, so typical of winter, is taken for granted as being part of our culture.

The fundamental physiological facts underpinning SAD cannot be dismissed so easily. The eyes are literally gateways to mind and body, taking in light, which triggers vital biological processes in the body – the ability to wake up and the ability to go to sleep, to name but two of the most basic. This waking and sleeping rhythm is one of the most profound of these processes – we live our lives by it.

Jacob Liberman describes the eyes as an extension of the brain and compares their immense complexity (they have more than a billion parts) to that of a space shuttle (with just 5.2 million parts). Unless we are partially sighted, around 90 per cent of the information we receive comes via the eyes. Of the three billion messages relayed to the brain every second, two billion are sent from the eyes. Our entire blood supply passes through our eyes every two hours and they use a third as much oxygen as the heart. Not just windows to the soul, but marvellously receptive sensing organs, our eyes are uniquely equipped to take in perhaps our most ignored nutrient – light.

The fact that light fluctuates with the seasons is so basic that we have forgotten about it. We are conscious of light and its waning at some level – hence depression and other symptoms when we are lacking it – but it is at the forefront of our thinking so we may not always realize just how much we need it. Yet, although to some extent we have lost touch with our seasonal nature, we remain seasonal beings.

CONCLUSION

It is hoped that this book – as well as raising consciousness about light and its absence in our lives – may offer more of a chance to enjoy the changing seasons and the positive aspects of winter. Enjoy an invigorating walk, the crisp beauty of a snowy day, hearty soups and stews, the cosiness of a fire. Above all, perhaps, winter offers the opportunity to relax, to slow down. The pressure is off and it can be soothing to go to bed early, stay home with the family or just be alone. The value of this 'hibernating' state is not to be underestimated, though it may often be denied by society. By following some of the suggestions in this book, you will find that a restful winter, allied to a new attitude to light, will leave you refreshed and ready for the more energetic demands of spring.

Further reading

Babbitt, Edwin, *Principles of Light and Colour*, New Jersey: Citadel 1967.

Cooper, Primrose, *The Healing Power of Light*, Piatkus 2000.

DesMaisons, Kathleen, *Potatoes Not Prozac*, New York: Simon & Schuster 1998.

Downing, Damien, *Day Light Robbery*, Arrow Books 1998.

Frazer, James, *The Golden Bough*, New York: Macmillan 1922; New York: Simon & Schuster 1996.

Hobday, Richard, *The Healing Sun*, Findhorn Press 2001.

Liberman, Jacob, *Light: Medicine of the Future*, Santa Fe, New Mexico: Bear & Company 1991; reprinted 1998.

Liberman, Jacob, *Take Off Your Glasses and See*, Thorsons 1995.

Liberman, Jacob, *Light Years Ahead* (1992 Conference Report), LYA Publications 1996.

Lorber, Jakob, *The Healing Power of Sunlight*, Merkur Publishing Company 1997.

Ott, John, *Health and Light: The effects of natural and artificial light on man and other living things*, Ariel Press 1976.

Ott, John, *My Ivory Cellar*, Chicago: Twentieth Century Press 1858; *Health and Light*, New York: Pocket Books 1973.

Rosenthal, Norman, *Winter Blues: Seasonal Affective Disorder – What It Is and How to Conquer It*, Fontana 1991.

Waterhouse, Debra, *From Tired to Inspired*, Thorsons 2000.

Zane, Kime, *Sunlight*, Penryn, California: World Health Publications 1980.

Useful addresses

The British Holistic Medical Association
59 Lansdowne Place
Hove
East Sussex BN3 1FL
Tel: 01273 725951
Website: www.bhma-sec.dircon.co.uk
E-mail: bhma@bhma.org

MIND (The National Association for Mental Health)
Granta House
15–19 Broadway
London E15 4BQ
Tel: 020 8519 2122
Website: www.mind.org.uk

The SAD Association (SADA)
PO Box 989
Steyning BN44 3HG
Website: www.sada.org.uk

Holistic resources
Website: www.holistic-online.com/hd_sad.htm

Health library
Website: www.internethealthlibrary.com/healthproblems/SAD.htm

Website: www.mentalhealth.com

Website: www.netdoctor.co.uk

Website: www.surgerydoor.co.uk

We Women
Website: www.WeWomen.co.uk

Light Therapy Equipment Suppliers

Bioptron Lamps
Glowing Health Distribution Ltd
Jayesforde House
College Road
Newton Abbot
Devon TQ12 1EF
Tel: 01626 526051

Boots
Larger branches may have lightboxes available.

Full-Spectrum Lighting
The SAD Box Company
Unit 1
Riverside Business Centre
Victoria Street
High Wycombe
Buckinghamshire HP11 2LT
Tel: 01494 526051

Outside In
Unit 21
Scotland Road
Dry Drayton
Cambridge CB3 8AT
Tel: 01954 211955
Website: www.outsidein.co.uk
E-mail: infa@outsidein.co.uk

Spectra-lite
York House
Lower Harlestone
Northampton NN7 4EW

The SAD Lighting Co. Ltd
19 Lincoln Road
Cressex Business Park
High Wycombe
Buckinghamshire HP12 3FX
Tel: 01494 448727/526051

USA

Ott-Light Systems
Environmental Lighting Concepts Inc.
3923 Coconut Palm Drive
101 Tampa
Florida
FL 33619
Tel: 001 813 621 0058

The Dinshah Health Society
100 Dinshah Drive
Malaga
New Jersey
NJ 08328

Universal Light Technology
President Jacob Liberman
PO Box 520
Carbondale
Colorado
CO 91623
Tel: 001 303 927 0100

BioBrite Inc
4350 East-West Highway
Suite 401-W
Bethseda
Maryland
MD 20814
Tel: 301 961 5960
Fax: 301 961 5943
E-mail: biobrite@ad.com

New Zealand
Elderhealth-Elderman
Dr Paul Goldshaw
Kaitemako Road, RD5
Tawanga
Tel: 0064 7544 0137
Fax: 0064 7544 0137
E-mail: ehew@xtra.co.nz

Germany
Hi Lite
Lomenstrasse 87
(Hamburg)
22869 Schenefeld
Tel: 40 220 4824
Fax: 40 227 5063
E-mail: rwlb@compuserve.com

Holland
Medilux
Postbus 28
52682G Helvoirtel 1967
Tel: 0411 642834
Fax: 0411 642655
E-mail: medilux@wx5.nl

Belgium
Elyzeese Velden 19
9000 Gent
Tel: 0032 9225 0226
Fax: 0032 9225 6492

Finland

Concreate Consulting Oy
Hiidentie 20
FIN-03250
Ojakkala
Tel: 358 40 55 20 185
Fax: 358 92 24 35 900
E-mail: conco@conco.fi

Astrids vei 3
1473 Skarer
Tel: 0047 6790 5555
Fax: 0047 6797 5155
E-mail: conco@conco.fi

Sweden

Bio-Britde Norden
Box 219 43225
Varberg
Tel: 0046 034067 1400
Fax: 0046 034067 1232
E-mail: bbn@varberg.se

Index